HOPE
against
HOPE

HOPE
against
HOPE

New Thinking In A Pigsty

Steve Mochechane

WestBow
PRESS
A DIVISION OF THOMAS NELSON

Scripture taken from the Holy Bible, New International Version®. Copyright © 1973, 1978, 1984 by International Bible Society. Used by permission of Zondervan. All rights reserved.

Scripture quotations marked TNIV are taken from the Holy Bible, Today's New International Version TM TNIV. ® Copyright © 2001, 2005 by International Bible Society®. All rights reserved worldwide.

Scripture quotations marked NLT are taken from the Holy Bible, New Living Translation, copyright © 1996, 2004. Used by permission of Tyndale House Publishers, Inc., Wheaton, Illinois 60189. All rights reserved.

Scripture quotations marked (The Message) are taken from The Message. Copyright © 1993, 1994, 1995, 1996, 2000, 2001, 2002. Used by permission of NavPress Publishing Group.

WestBow Press books may be ordered through booksellers or by contacting:

WestBow Press
A Division of Thomas Nelson
1663 Liberty Drive
Bloomington, IN 47403
www.westbowpress.com
1-(866) 928-1240

Because of the dynamic nature of the Internet, any web addresses or links contained in this book may have changed since publication and may no longer be valid. The views expressed in this work are solely those of the author and do not necessarily reflect the views of the publisher, and the publisher hereby disclaims any responsibility for them.

Any people depicted in stock imagery provided by Thinkstock are models, and such images are being used for illustrative purposes only.

Certain stock imagery © Thinkstock.

ISBN: 978-1-4497-3559-3 (sc)

Library of Congress Control Number: 2011963201

Printed in the United States of America

WestBow Press rev. date: 03/05/2012

DEDICATION

In memory of Gertrude Masabata Mochechane—hope transferred.
Dedicated to our children Obakeng and Khumo—hope inferred, and
to the glory of Christ our Lord—hope preferred.

Jürgen Moltmann:

I don't dispute that others find courage for life and the power of suffering elsewhere. But for me this courage and power come again and again when I hold before me the picture of Christ. His passion for life led him to suffering on the cross. It is in his passion and his suffering that the passion of God becomes clear to me, and it is from God's passion that I receive the power to resist death.

CONTENTS

FOREWORD

I first met Steve some years ago at Garret Evangelical in Evanston, Illinois. At the time we were the only two students from Southern Africa studying at the seminary, and naturally we shared a lot about home over many African dishes prepared by my wife Bertha.

Reminiscing about home we often got personal, and many of the experiences he shares in this book we discussed, especially some of the episodes from his first marriage. It's been more than twenty years since, and I was surprised to hear from him recently—still wrestling with issues of personal anxiety.

For me, one thing stands out; his tenacious spirit to hope against hope. Steve's story is not unique; we each travel down the road of anxiety in some sense, how we walk down that road though is something else. Some win where others have lost, and some lose where others have won. While we can learn from others who went before us, the journey always unfolds differently for each person.

Nothing lures like hope, Martin Luther King had a dream, and Mandela was driven by an "ideal" of a just and democratic South Africa. Steve dares for us to hope again! Hope comes in many directions, and often our expectations are crushed. In this book we are encouraged to hope in God through Christ; it is not a religious thing, it is a matter between life and death.

A unique feature in this book is that the author writes for him before he writes for others, because nothing teaches like experience. While extensive consultation was made with a variety of relevant resources, Steve succeeds in being his own psychotherapist. His story is told in chunks of ten. Each ten years is a reflection of how the past has impacted the present. The story is an interesting biography of learning. The best way to move forward is to learn not to repeat one's mistakes, and to improve on one's strengths.

Here is yet another testament to the invincibility of the human spirit. I hope readers will find it as inspiring and moving to action as I did. If you feel trapped in some human travesty, prepare to move on. Steve's work is an example of how we each can reflect on our own stories, and then use that as a platform to come out of our graves. The way things have been, is not the way things can be!

Dr. Tapiwa Mucherera
Professor of Pastoral Counseling
Asbury Theological Seminary
Wilmore, Kentucky

PROLOGUE

This book had no choice but to be written. So much emotional churning was going on; had it not been written, I would have literally exploded. I've tried to capture in readable form the many directions of the tensions and contradictions of a dialogue with God within my soul.

The African Bishop of Hippo inspired this initiative. I read *The Confessions of St. Augustine* vociferously, stunned by how a man could be so bluntly candid, transparent and open with God. In my religious background, God was the unforgiving consuming fire, ready to rain sulphur and brimstone at first offence—you had to be careful about what you said. In the tradition of the psalmists, St. Augustine spoke to God about anything and everything.

Like the Bishop, these are my confessions, perhaps written differently, but they speak to the heart of issues I've wrestled with over many years. Here, I expose my own nakedness. It's been a long, scary, and arduous journey, but worth every mile. The initiative is likely to solicit more scorn than sympathy from some quarters; but that is not why it was written. Instead, I extend a helping hand to someone travelling down what M. Scott Peck called, *"The Road Less Travelled."*

It may seem strange that I begin my story with the last part. I can only say that the end of a story is always better than the beginning. Essentially, this is not an autobiography in the traditional sense; it is a pilgrimage of learning, and a shifting of paradigms—frozen patterns of thinking entrenched by time.

I narrate my story in overlapping interconnections, from early childhood well into adulthood. Sometimes I am direct, honest and straightforward, other times I leave it to the reader to fill in the blanks by reflecting on their own story in the context of my journey.

Initially I wrote primarily for catharsis, not publication. Only later in the journey did I realise that personal stories were turning my life around. I share my story not because it is unique, but because in the travesty of what I was, I discovered the unfolding person I didn't know I could become.

My religious roots, carved in 19th century "holiness" tradition, insisted on human perfection, and the reality on the ground was very different. The harder I tried to be spotless, the more I failed; I was driven into despair and intense emotional and psychological conflict. Something was wrong: either the map, or the territory.

St. Augustine's *Confessions* were a great psychological breakthrough; there is no such thing as a perfect human being—that is why Christ died on the cross. Human nature is flawed on every level, and our deliverance is found and perfected only in the event on the cross, and the unfolding process of the work of the Spirit. Going back and forth in dialogue with the *Confessions,* my crisis of the conscience was slowly but surely being resolved.

Viktor Frankl (1984) initiated me into Logotherapy. While I am of the opinion that he didn't go far enough, he triggered an interest in me to study in a deeper sense the concept of the Logos, especially as presented in the Gospel and epistles of John the apostle.

Frankl is either "half full" or "half empty". He admits that the religious experiences of some Nazi prisoners were useful in helping them maintain sanity under gruelling circumstances, but religious experience in this context is nothing more than a positive thinking tool, and in that sense he is half full. He didn't take God all the way—in his therapy, God is a device in the practice of psychiatry, not the Living God espoused by biblical scripture.

The half-empty side of the Logotherapy coin is where Frankl insists that an ideal worth living for is enough to keep one going, and here he quotes Nietzsche more frequently. While some of it is psychologically valid and empirically verifiable, I think it turns the fabrications of the human mind into an idol, and it fits perfectly with Nietzsche's existential thinking: *"There is no God; if there were, how would I stand it if I were not him."* Either way, Logotherapy does not do sufficient justice to the concept of the Logos.

Ironically, this Frankl context provided me with the dialectic framework in which my theology began to make deeper sense. Personally, I find it impossible to think anything without the eternal living God as my ultimate frame of reference—where does one start? It seems limiting, but this was the precise point of my liberation in every direction. Spreading is easier if you have a starting point, and for me that point is the Christ of God. In his eternalness, he goes beyond my limitations.

For me the eternalness of God suggests that God will never be captured, or understood satisfactorily or fully within the limitations of the human mind. It is this aspect of God that makes revelation necessary, and for the follower of Christ, that revelation is captured fully in the Logos.

I am a follower of Christ, even though others have challenged the credibility of my Christ experience, either because I do not measure up to their moral fabrications, or because I do not subscribe to the mental picture of the Christ they hold. I am a follower of Christ simply because I have accepted his life on earth, his death on the cross and his resurrection as the pinnacle of God's gesture of reconciliation towards humanity. That admission is my fate, and it gives meaning and direction to my life here on earth—it is the very essence of my passion for life. It is in Christ that I ultimately see and experience the invincibility of the human spirit.

St. Augustine gave me the psychology; Frankl, the theology; and Peter Senge (1990) gave me the technology to convert theory into practice. His theory on learning organisations enabled me to revise my tired religious models, and to search deep in my own spirit for what I was passionate about.

This is a journey of memories, largely because I wanted to gain clues into my own personality. It is not possible to remember every valley or mountaintop in one's life experience, but certain things stand out as unforgettable and contribute in significant ways to events that shaped one's personality. Leo Tolstoy had only four memories before the age of 5, but that's no reason to give up.

I open me up to the reader purely to facilitate the beginning of an arduous process of "physician heal thyself." We each have a story to tell, and while most people would find it comfortable to bury theirs, not much healing takes place. Telling your own story is not only therapeutic; it gives you the opportunity to start again.

In Part 1, I dare to confront my "ghosts." I didn't even know I had them, but the reflection provided me with an opportunity to think deeply about my situation. I didn't think I deserved to be in so much pain, what then was I doing in this emotional hellhole? I think it's a good place to start, because nobody knows you like you do. It is also your leverage in staging a powerful comeback. People may say all kinds of things about you, but they don't hold as much power over you as you do over yourself. I came out with one lesson in this exercise; the best way to cripple your way forward is to blame other people for your situation.

Part 2 is where the real work began, my biggest problem was not my situation, but how I saw or thought about it. It's not an overnight thing, and the process is still unfolding; but the initial steps had a healing I could not explain. My future depended on my attitude. It's amazing what we drag along in the environments that shape our thinking. My childhood wasn't very exciting, but I didn't think it could help me move forward. There is a lot that happened back then that influenced my images of life. I had to bring most of it back; either revise the models, or discard them. There were no shortcuts, it all had to be done step by meticulous step.

In Part 3 I reflect on how each one of us is finger-print unique. It was very liberating to know that I had the right to be me. And that I could still become who God has created for me to be. Remaining in the rut was not doing anybody a favour, I had to come out, and explore my own gifts.

Part 4 explores the question of hope. This is nothing about wishful thinking, or building castles in the air; it is hope in God through Christ. It is here that my Christ experience became very meaningful. It wasn't enough to work on the transformation of my mind; I had to start hoping again, and to make sure that my hope was anchored in God. Again this called for a revision of my religious models; keeping what worked, and throwing out what didn't. My religious background placed more emphasis on hope "in the sweet by and by." In so many ways I heard about the kingdom of God, but that did not have any implications for everyday life. I had to die first, or be caught up in the air before I could enjoy God. Nothing around me said things can be different right here on earth.

The epilogue is my struggle with fear. I was afraid to move out and to move on. It took me a while to put together the courage, but I finally did. Hope was calling, and like Lazarus, I took my first steps out. A thousand miles begin with the first step.

1

CONFRONTING THE TRUTH

If you want to know me;
Then you must know my story,
For my story defines who I am.
If I want to know myself,
To gain insight into the meaning of my life,
Then I, too, must come to know my story.

Dan McAdams

"*The map is not the territory,*" people say, and it's true. Unless the map keeps up with the territory, it runs the risk of being outdated. Since 1994 the map of South Africa has changed drastically; many people woke up one morning and found themselves on the wrong side of the border. Territories are unpredictable, and usually it is easier adapting the map to the territory instead of the other way around.

The excitement of any journey is not the destination but the road; seeing the trees, the mountains, the natural scenery, and many firsts that you never thought of, or even knew existed. As you travel the journey—not some fabrication of the mind—the map begins to adjust to the reality on the ground.

Life is a journey between birth and death, and we do not have the luxury of choosing when, where and how it happens. We are thrown into it, and thrown out in the end. As we go through the journey, we experience life as it is, not as we imagine it to be. It will negotiate terms with us, or us with it; and all of that depends on where we stand in relation to God—seeing God from a human perspective, or seeing life from a God perspective.

THE WOUNDED HEALER

M. Scott Peck (1978) began his book, *The Road Less Travelled,* with a simple assertion: *"Life is difficult"*. That is as given as a mathematical formula; it's like saying, *"the ocean is full of water"*. If you want to live in that environment, you build a ship, learn how to swim, walk on water, or become a shark. You can't cry the ocean dry. If you are going to live this life, then you have to learn how.

When you are tiptoeing on the edges of adversity, you want the environment to change, only to discover much later that real change begins with you. Mahatma Ghandi was right: *"Be the change you want to see."* You may be the most difficult thing to work with, but it's always the best place to start.

This is a story of a painful episode in my life, a snippet of transition and transformation in a drama that continues to play on. It is the story of Kingdom nuggets I learned in limbo. In mid-air a still small voice spoke to me, *Jeremiah 36:2 "Take a scroll and write on it all the words I have spoken to you . . ."* Learning was the heart of this whole thing—it couldn't have come any other way.

I'd spent almost forty years of my life under apartheid, and it was natural to blame it for every detail of my problems, but now apartheid was gone, and I had nothing and no one to blame. I could have invented other alternatives if I wanted to: family curses, witchcraft, or some other gory thing to make my troubles seem more authentic. In Africa nothing just happens—something, or someone, brought it on you; you just never do it all by yourself. The finger-pointing syndrome is all too widespread when things don't seem to be working out.

That trend of thinking had to go, because it empowered circumstances I couldn't control. I had to nail the problem and my relationship to it. I missed the point where I was the sinner, and for a while, I missed the opportunity to turn the situation around. John the apostle gave me the wake-up call, *1John 1:10* *"If we claim we have not sinned, we make him out to be a liar and his word has no place in our lives."*

That was very powerful, it forced me to pull my finger back, and identify the places where I missed the mark. It is easier to blame others for our own misery, but it is disabling. You miss the opportunity to be hurt by your own pain, and chances are you will repeat the mistake, because only a burnt child dreads fire.

Turning the searchlight on ourselves is an excruciating process, yet it is the pain that lays the groundwork for our healing. An effective healer is a wounded one, and the Christ of God led the way along this path, *Hebrews 2:18* *"Because he himself suffered when he was tempted, he is able to help those who are being tempted."*

I had to step out of myself, and observe myself from the point of a total stranger. Mandela says a pivotal moment of his stay in prison was the ability to transcend himself. No personal change is possible without some degree of rising above ourselves. In fact, genuine transformation is a journey of personal transcendence and transformation, not so much on the outside as it must be on the inside.

Every appliance comes with a manual, and every manual has a troubleshooting section. Somewhere deep in my subconscious, it was entrenched that I am created in the image of God, and that began a very fascinating relationship with the bible. I looked at myself from the manual perspective: was I functioning optimally and according to specification and design? The more I examined biblical scriptures in relation to where I stood, the more my flaws were exposed.

Hard times are meaningful when we learn from them, whether we bring them on ourselves, or whether they are brought on us by others, or circumstances beyond our control. Sometimes we go through adversity to be able to comfort others. Looking back, I wouldn't trade my experiences for the world—indeed, like Samson, whose sweetness came from the carcass of a dead lion, I learned more from adversity than all my schooling years put together. The apostle Paul was right, *2 Corinthians 1:4 (NLT)* *"He comforts us in all our troubles so that we can comfort others. When they are troubled, we will be able to give them the same comfort God has given us."* Experience is still the best teacher!

IN SEARCH OF A USABLE PAST

When I started writing this chronicle, I sat in a packed and dark Zozo[1] structure at the back of my mother's house and revisited a journey to where I did not want to go. I reflected on the story of my past, and something opened up inside of me, a thin golden lining of hope under a very heavy cloud.

Jeremiah 36:2 launched my writing career. I responded to the challenge because it offered hope just when I thought the world had run out of fuel. God spoke to me in my pain, and I caught it on paper. Suddenly a task lay before me that had the potential to last a lifetime—I had a reason to live!

Starting a writing career at fifty—wasn't that a little too ambitious? Some people thought so, but everything else around me disagreed. It seemed a long way off, but the first steps had to be taken. It took me about five years to go through some thirty years of raw material—the

---

[1]   Zozo structures are a form of below-the-breadline accommodation found in the backyard of most "matchbox" houses in South African townships.

first time I had consistently stayed with anything for that long, and I loved every minute of it. I had discovered my passion.

It dawned on me that none of us is here merely as a product of sexual indulgence between two people; there is more to it, much, much more. We are not just isolated beings on earth, but we are part of God's greater purpose in an unfolding universe. Every star is meant to shine its own shine. My star wasn't burnt out yet; it just had to be led to its rightful place among many. The world would be a different place if we all found our spot in the *divine* scheme of things; Jesus called it *seeking the Kingdom of God*.

Life is all about choices, good or bad; as Steven Covey (1989:69-70) says, between stimulus and response, we are given the power to choose. I chose badly, and sometimes with a clear conscience, but that sad story was about to change. The choice was mine to make, and that choice introduced the moment of my liberation. The point was simple and succinct; we choose what we become.

Inside me, something opened up to the spirit of the eternal *divine*. Suddenly my spirit had access to a reservoir I could never exhaust. It felt like an endless supply of freshness, with every sip better than the one before. I developed a very deep sense of God-consciousness. Biblical scripture and its often unexplored images came alive and in a small yet powerful way, I drew from the eternal Christ and the power of his resurrection.

GOD IS IN CHARGE!

One dark night I stood staring at the stars above, and it suddenly struck me that they just hang there sustained by the Creator. Some scientists refuse to credit God with the awesomeness of God's creation.

Maybe there was a "big bang", but that should explain the genius of a God who can create order out of chaos, a God who was there before the chaotic explosion out of which the universe was born. I was dealing with my own "big bang", and my chaos was no exception.

I am convinced that God was at work behind the chaotic scenes in my life, just as God is in everything else. For some people, Adam Smith's economic "invisible hand" is easier to believe than God's hidden hand in ordering human experience, but God is involved, much more than we are willing to admit or realise.

No one sees the forces of gravity with the naked eye, but we know they are at work, because whatever goes up must come down. We know that the earth is magnetic because the compass is always pointing north. Eventually, life links up in complex and intricate ways, we must climb without a ladder in a universe where everything is suspended and God holds it all together. The Spirit of God hovers over the chaos and ultimately gives meaning to human existence. It is the voice of God that pronounces creative and new beginnings, *"Let there be . . ."*

When God created the human being, he said, ^{Genesis 1:26(TNIV)} "Let us make human beings in our image, in our likeness, and let them rule over the fish of the sea and the birds of the air, over the livestock, over all the earth, and over all the creatures that move along the ground."

We were created, not to *be* God, but to be *like* God, and to call into existence things that are not as if they were, and to create order out of chaos. The cliché still applies: like begets like. Paul wrote, ^{Acts 17:28} *"For in him we live and move and have our being. As some of your own poets have said, 'We are his offspring.'"*

A still small voice said inside of me, *"You are more powerful that you think".* All I could see at the time were the mountains of problems that surrounded me. I could not figure a way out at all; then Paul's words to the Corinthians came to mind, ^{1Cointhians 10:13 (TNIV)} *"No temptation has overtaken you except what is common to us all. And God is faithful; he will not let you be tempted beyond what you can bear. But when you are tempted, he will also provide a way out so that you can endure it."*

CAUGHT PANTS-DOWN, OFF-GUARD

The drama of my misery began with the loss of a job, a house and our cars, and reached its peak with the loss of my wife; all of that in a swirling tornado of events brutally spinning out of control, and within a very short space of time.

When we left Machadodorp (200 km east of Johannesburg) in 2003, we had no idea what was in store for us. We were coming back home to Johannesburg after an absence of more than ten years, and as we landed, we were hit in the face by a ton of misfortunes we least expected—caught pants-down totally off-guard.

If you are knocked off your feet like that, you wonder why you didn't see it coming. But that's like trying to control an act of nature. Some things may be predictable, but they are way beyond our control. If you survive, you can only watch as they rip through structures created by human hands. Sometimes you are swept along in a roaring, raging and rolling mudslide uprooting everything down a twisty rugged and rocky mountain path.

By the time my storm was through with me, I was emotionally and psychologically bruised. It hurt like nothing I'd ever known before. I had all the time in the world to die or to live again; and I chose to live again. It was the beginning of another journey. I took myself apart piece by piece; it was the only way I would get to know how I got to be where I was.

I began a journey into myself as if I was braving the dense jungles of the Amazon. I had to separate the wood from the trees, and through the woods, I discovered Kingdom secrets, great and small. For a while, I could not identify the new person I was becoming; "Where have I been?" I asked with a freshness I didn't know existed. The kind you feel like a breeze in a scorching hot desert.

The beauty of searching oneself is that one must be thoroughly honest with oneself. How do you hide from yourself? The bigger challenge was to confront my skeletons; they'd been in the closet too long. The stink was overwhelming, but it was my stink. I had to let go, and let the Spirit of God permeate my innermost; it guaranteed my healing. David wrote, *Psalm 139:23* *"Search me, O God, and know my heart; test me and know my anxious thoughts."*

God has a way of being eloquent and crystal clear in our pain. Job said, *Job 36:15* *"But those who suffer he delivers in their suffering; he speaks to them in their affliction."* The birthing pains of newness are excruciating but when the new life is born, we guard it with the jealousy of a leopard watching over her young.

We love complexity, even though we coil ourselves with it. That is the point where Adam and Eve where thrown into a whirlwind of anxiety. God made life simple, and all they had to do was work the garden, and God would take care of providence. The challenge of life is simple, if we do our best with what we have been given. Life itself is a gift, if we receive him who came that we might have life to the fullest.

Curiosity and greed made it more complex, and right there our anxiety was born. They lost a whole garden for one tree. Sometimes we cry out for what we can't have, only to lose what we have—or worse still, what we didn't even know we had—the kingdom of God within us. God in and with us, ready to invade the earth in a new way.

I discovered increasingly that life is in fact all about climbing without a ladder because nothing in the universe is permanent or sure, except faith, hope and love. Things slip even with the toughest grip. We march up and down human existence wearing a pretext of slippery confidence, only to land ourselves in the quicksand of self-deception. When all is said and done, God is in charge.

WHAT IS THE MEANING OF MY LIFE?

My inward journey was both healing and educational. It gave me the opportunity to grieve and to regurgitate and reflect on a rough ride I had neither anticipated nor planned. Above all, I set out on a new path to redefine the purpose of my life; Frankl (1984) called it *"the will to meaning"*. It began with the question: What is the meaning of my life?

I had asked that question before, but not as deeply as I felt it now. There had to be a reason for living beyond the dictates of the five senses, and the temporary fortifications of the environment. My decisive moment had arrived, and in some urgent way I had to make constructive sense out of my misery. "What does it all mean?" It had to be done, otherwise I would have died, literally locked in some elaborate timber case and buried in a dark cold grave somewhere.

My wife suffered asthma attacks. One evening as she lay in hospital, I sent her a text message on my cell phone, *"Don't die on my children!"* I didn't know what else to say, because I was intensely afraid, and that was my most chronic fear. By some sixth sense I knew something extreme was waiting to happen. She died on 28 March 2006; and nothing had ever hit me between the eyes like that. It took a while to sink.

When my brother told me about her death, I felt a great amount of strength leave me. Deep inside a big chunk of me sank; I felt like a pound of flesh had just been butchered off my body without sympathy. Our struggles were now irreversible.

When Gerty's sister confirmed her death, I just hung up the phone and broke into tears, in broad daylight in a central business area. Something good had been emerging about my wife and I . . . and she took it with her. The greatest difficulty on the face of the earth was to tell my children Obakeng and Khumo that their mother had passed on. What would I say, how would I begin? At ages 11 and 8, it just wasn't fair on them. But eventually it had to come out. I had to get hold of them as quickly as possible. I phoned the school and arranged to pick them up earlier than usual. My greatest fear had just descended on us.

OB thought I had it all wrong, "Papa, are you sure?" He kept asking because their maternal grandfather had passed away a few days earlier. We took turns comforting each other.

During the funeral service I didn't know how to feel. She lay next to her father, as if to deny him the pleasure or pain of journeying into eternity alone. I pushed my way through the funeral programme just to convince myself I needed closure. I stuttered some throat-choking claptrap and just cried.

My kids and I stood by her graveside, dumbfounded, as we said our final goodbyes. Nobody felt our pain, nobody could; we had to take it as raw as it was given to us. We shared the pain of her loss in different ways; I wanted to take it all away, especially for my children—but how do you take away pain like that? The world would be an empty place without Ma-Gert. Our pain moved to a different level altogether.

Ma-Gert was gone—as in no return—and all that remained with us was reminiscences and memories—the good times, and the bad. For more than ten years all four of us were inseparable, and now one of us was gone; so quickly and unexpectedly. Just when we thought we would never be separated again. We had travelled together on every occasion to the distant places where we lived; the four of us was all we had. Now it was over, shattered and broken into irretrievable pieces.

Gerty had not been ready to go because she loved life with a passion. She would have wanted to see her kids grow, see them through school, and perhaps live to see their children. Like most of us, she was a dreamer of big dreams. For the most part, she gave some up for our family.

My kids had to stay with their maternal grandmother because I had no place to live, and I was left all alone. My mind raced back to my first marriage: I could not be part of my older son's life from when he was 8 or 10 years old, and here I was away from my children again; was this some kind of generational curse or what?

I didn't grow up with my father, and all my young life I vowed that my kids would never grow up without me. I have five children and none of them has grown up around me, or been with me for long enough. With a hundred thoughts of evil running through my mind, the ground beneath my feet gradually opened up . . .

I went away from the cemetery bitterly angry; I was angry with Gerty and I was angry with me. I thought of all the good and bad times we had, and the many ways we both let the enemy in over the years; those chickens had finally come home to roost.

I looked around at friend and foe alike; it was as if everybody was saying, "You got what you deserved." One woman had a big smile on her face, as if to say, "Good shot!" But a friend drove many kilometres to be by my side, a gesture I will never forget.

I struggled to swallow my bitter pill, our twelve years of blight and bliss ended rather harsh and abruptly. It was not easy dealing with her passing away, but I drew some comfort in knowing that at least one part of our vows had been kept: "Till death us do part."

SHIFTING SHADOWS MOVE NORTH

We arrived in Musina in 1994, just a few months after our marriage, and less than six months after I came out of a very adolescent, chaotic and embarrassing marriage. I spent ten painful years in that first relationship and had nothing to show for it except a loving son whose life I could never be a part of. I was emotionally drained, inside out and upside down; I needed much more than a pastoral sabbatical (or so I thought), and Musina was ideal—it was almost 600 km north from the things that caused me pain and where I caused pain. As a pastor, you help others through their pain and anguish, but often, you are left alone to tread your own road.

I hit the ceiling, and not knowing where else to turn I took the road headed north. Abraham went south to Egypt; Jonah went to Tarshish; and I went north to Musina, literally at the border of South Africa and Zimbabwe.

Working for an excellent diamond mine was just what I needed. Earning my money felt good, very good. It was an opportunity to begin a new life in a totally different and hopefully more peaceful context, new family, new job, new people; I was literally shutting the doors behind me, and looking forward to new opportunities. Ministry was not cutting it for me; and I just wanted my life back.

Life in Musina was the closest I ever came to a stable family life, the usual dream family of husband, wife, two children, a boy and a girl. For more than ten years I woke up every day with my wife next to me, and sleepy children looking forward and waiting to take a shower with their dad; and later being driven to school or nursery school.

My previous marriage was not only adolescent; it was permanently disabled by apartheid. In fact, I have no memories of it. I was on a constant flight from pillar to post, avoiding security police or confronting apartheid in my hometown, and the situation never got a fair start.

UNLESS YOU WATCH YOURSELF, NOBODY'S WATCHING YOU

Musina was an opportunity to establish myself in a totally new field. As a pastor I was a people's person, so human resources was appropriate I suppose. My interests in the management sciences were sparked during my graduate studies in Evanston, Illinois. So here I was, in the HR department in a De Beers mine, and the move took care of all the little concerns I had as a pastor.

For once I had decent housing, medical aid, my kids could go to a private school, and I could afford a new car and a different lifestyle. The first two levels of Maslow's hierarchy were taken care of; I was not bothered by not being in so-called full-time ministry, part of me was bored with the unchallenging and monotonous chores of the usual pastoral routine anyway.

Life offers different alternatives; it can be much more exciting and challenging out there, but it can be unpleasant too. Achievement without character is like freedom without a charter, you tend to abuse the goodness of life because you think it was created for you. That is how free I felt . . . From then on, I was going to do it my way!

Somehow, I ended up pastoring a church in that distant place, but even then, it was pastoring on my own terms. For some reason, I could not shake off the pastor in me. It kept following me even in places where I wanted to bury it—someone would just sniff me out.

"NOT FROM AROUND HERE ARE YOU?"

The prodigal son in a land far away must have felt the same way, "I am in charge of me! I owe nobody an explanation about anything!" The reckless young man had his own money, he did not have to depend on his father anymore, and he went on a riotous spending spree.

That is the peril of freedom in a faraway land; you suddenly become the vortex of your own vex and vice because nobody's watching. You live as if there's no tomorrow, and when tomorrow comes you are caught sitting by the side of the road with very limited choices; even pig food becomes a rare and delicious dish.

Your soul steadily begins to empty and your spiritual perspectives take on a slow but sure blur. You are full but you are empty, and usually there are no red flags to warn you when the thick ice beneath your feet grows thinner. Unless you watch yourself, nobody is really watching you.

If you lose your head in careless living, you could break your neck. Some situations don't give you a second chance. In a distant land, nobody knows you and nobody cares! You are on your own, and forever "not from around here are you?" If you die out there, you are just another statistic lying by the side of the road. Everybody goes on with business as usual as if nothing happened.

SHIFTING SHADOWS MOVE SOUTH

After almost ten years in Musina, we decided to come back to Gauteng. I continued working in the corporate world, first as a human resources generalist for a poultry company, and then as the human resources development manager for a chrome smelter in Mpumalanga. Life continued as usual until our currency started gaining strength against the American dollar in late 2003. Usually that is bad news for mining and related industries. They do most of their business abroad and rely heavily on a stronger dollar against a weaker rand; in short, they make more money if our currency is weaker.

Our company (like many others) was forced to cut down on its workforce, and guess who had to go first: the highest paid in the training department. My makeshift world began to sink, and slowly but surely, the quicksand drew me in.

I bought a new car in August, and was retrenched in September; nobody wanted to know what would happen to my kids or me. Someone had to make a smart "business decision" for the company and I was it. I was not even allowed back into the office the next day. They called it "protecting company property and information". That was it—I was out! It was as if someone was waiting for it to happen.

Just a day earlier, I thought I was the blue-eyed boy of the situation, I did not even think it possible that things would change. I felt a big wound in my back, like Caesar, it took a while before I realised I had a Brutus in my crowd. Someone had been waiting for the opportunity. The most effective blow usually comes from the inner circle.

It was such a weighty punch; it left me heavily gasping for breath for months. Whatever trust I had in time, people and events took a deep plunge. I thought I was going to die. Everything was happening so quickly, I just had to put on a mask of strength just to pretend it was not so bad. In a fake world, you can't show everybody that the wheels are coming off; folks enjoy it when you are thrown into a deep hole. I was sliding fast to where I didn't want to go.

Perhaps it was not so bad, I still thought I could look for a job and curb the misery. I applied, attended interviews, borrowed money, spoke to friends in high places, sold a few household items, but nothing worked. A cousin suggested it was time to consult my ancestors; that was a very appealing proposal.

To hell and back

Things got worse, I put every cent I had towards securing a bank loan for a house; after all, I was going to go vigorous job-hunting and everything would soon fall back into place; or so I thought. I ran hysterically hard, and in the process, the court sheriff kept demanding and auctioning one item at a time until everything was gone. What he did not sell I sold, and for the first time in many years we lived from hand to mouth.

My kids were frustrated, they were young and perhaps too naive to understand what was going on; they had never had to live that way before. I carried Khumo to school on my back, and we went through biting winter mornings in a wide-open farming area with her brother following close beside us. The distances were too long to walk. That was a drastic change from the life they knew, and she kept moaning, "Maybe we should go back to Machadodorp." She thought it was the territory that brought us so much misery.

We had about seventeen sheep on the small farm. They too became a luxury we could not afford, and the more we ran out of food and money, the quicker they had to go; either sold or eaten. My sick, old and helpless blind father kept complaining and calling for attention when we least could afford it. Eventually, I took him back home; and at the time Zimbabwe was not the right place to return a sick and blind old man; we both knew he was driven back there to die . . . He said as much just after a rare fill of hot fish and chips beyond the Limpopo River.

The situation weighed heavily on all of us and in no time, our marriage relationship took a nosedive. My wife could not take it anymore, she left, and I plunged into a deep depression.

A hundred, maybe a thousand, thoughts ran through my mind . . . In the bigger picture, it was a trying time for all of us. When you hit rock bottom, the options for self-destruction are many—suicide, drugs, alcohol and many more. You end up with a gaping and painful choking thing on your throat that you don't know what to do with. It's like someone just poured your soul full of sulphuric acid, and you feel the flesh peeling off in the most excruciating pain you have ever felt.

The hardest thing is to see everything you lived and worked for suddenly fall into little pieces you cannot save right before your very eyes, it's like your very soul is squeezed out of you and you suddenly become a living yet lifeless bag of bones ready for cremation. People see you smile, and yet deep inside you walk the walk of another aching mile.

Where was God in all of this? I'd never been pushed this far in all my life, and if God was out there somewhere, I needed him desperately and immediately! In some way, my faith in Christ had to start making serious sense. How relevant was it to my pain; even more serious: how was I going to get out of this rut?

TERROR ON EVERY SIDE!

Jeremiah the prophet once complained, ^{Jeremiah 20:10(NLT)} *"I hear many whispering, 'Terror on every side! Report him! Let us report him!' All my friends are waiting for me to slip, saying, 'Perhaps he will be deceived; then we will prevail over him and take our revenge on him.'"* I felt so alone in a frantic universe spinning at an overwhelming speed. Me against the world!

The prodigal son's money ran out about the exact time famine came to the land. Strange coincidence we might say, but in God's bigger picture, every detail of our lives is designed to fit into the mysterious evolution and synergy of the universe. Everything happens according to God's overall and total plan.

The young man was hit suddenly and without warning; he had no food, no place to live, no family, no friends and no money; those crucial things that drive humanity's motivation for survival. His esteem and fame shot down below zero in no time. Everything he took for granted was wiped out in one definite strike.

Sometimes we complacently enjoy the goodness of life as if things are meant to go on forever; and then the earth turns on its axis, and the bright side becomes dark—very dark. The young man became the stranger in a foreign land that he really was, and that pompous aura of playing big in a small town proved unsustainable after all.

It is hard to beg when you are not used to it, but some lessons must be taken even if it means swallowing your pride, and they become clearer in the most grave of places, just where you don't want to be. If you don't swallow your arrogance, it will choke its way down your throat anyway. The boy ended up in a pigsty, something he never thought possible, and there was no turning back.

Adversity has a tendency to ambush; it does not give the slightest hint of what is about to happen in the next step that you are about to take. Things can be slippery in the snowy slopes of life; you fall even when you are a maestro skating on thick ice. You may even start an avalanche rolling.

RIP VAN WINKLE SLEPT FOR TWENTY YEARS IN THE MOUNTAINS

When I came out of my "Rip van Winkle" spell almost two years later, there was nothing and nobody around me except my children. Everyone I lived with on the small farm was dead, stone dead, and that was just overwhelming. My father died of hunger in a remote village in Zimbabwe with no one to care for him, my wife's heart and lungs gave up, and my cousin died in a car accident and his body lay for hours by the side of the road before any assistance came. It felt like a roller coaster ride into the bosom of hell and back.

When I decided to come down from the mountain of despondency the landscape had changed dramatically. It was the same place, yet different. I was reminded again of the prodigal son; scripture says, *Luke 15:17 "When he came to his senses"*. By implication, he was out of his senses when he made the decisions that landed him in the pigsty. I had to start asking some soul-probing questions: how did I get to be where I was, how was I related to my problem, or was destiny just taking a wrong turn on me?

17

My mind raced up and down my past; where did it all go wrong? I could see how some choices I made were returning to haunt me. Now wasn't a good time, but the chickens were here to roost. Out-of-sense decisions have a way of landing us in the quagmire, especially if made within the context of the small picture; every decision we make has far-reaching implications even though the fuller pattern is not yet clear.

So often we are caught up in the "now" of our situation, and consider very little of the "not yet". We learn in small and big ways that no decision is made in isolation; some immediate decisions may provide temporary relief but they run miles ahead to ambush you later and in the most unexpected and unwelcome of places. Today's problems are always born from yesterday's solutions.

PURPOSE IS BURIED DEEP IN OUR EMPTINESS

Life has a way of sitting you down until you learn that it owes you nothing. It waits patiently for you to return the investment buried deep in you. As Frankl (1984:131) observed, *"Ultimately, man should not ask what the meaning of his life is, but rather he must recognise it is he who is asked."*

Sometimes we ask for the meaning of life as if someone must give it to us on a silver platter. We live life as if it owes us a good turn and we are disappointed when it unfolds differently. That was a hard pill to swallow; I didn't ask to be born. It didn't matter now; I was born, and the question was for what?

For the first time in a very long time, I started wrestling with questions of purpose. "What on earth am I here for?" I had to look that question straight in the eye, or die! Rick Warren's book, *The purpose driven life* hit South African bookshelves right on time. Nothing was new; I just was astounded by its simple and yet profound message—Life is about God.

My biggest problem was relational; God was God for me. I kept asking, "Wasn't God here to serve my purpose and to make me prosper?"

Everywhere else in religion, people summon God into their activities, and then walk away into business as usual. I couldn't see me in relation to God's greater cosmic purpose—the Kingdom of God purpose. We are born to prosper God's purpose; and ours is prospered in his own— that left me feeling even emptier and yet fuller at the same time.

While wrestling with Warren's statement, something whispered in my spirit, *"Empty is the place to be if you must be filled with God."* I was reminded of a science teacher who held up a glass with "nothing" in it and asked, "What's in this glass?" We all shouted back confidently, "Nothing!" With a smile he retorted, "There's air in this glass my children, air; you just cannot see or smell it."

Another truth hit me; empty spaces are full if we learn how to look and to see beyond the ordinary. Just because you cannot see or smell does not mean it is not happening. Some things are not visible to the human eye, and some smells are odourless. There is a lot of unseen activity going on in the universe verified by scientific research, and the delusion that reality is based only on the five senses has long been laid to rest.

Out there, space is filled with the most astounding artistic creativity and design, and everything is playing out and fulfilling the purpose for which it was created. In fact, there is no such thing as empty space because every space is filled with the possibility of newness. There is a lot of chaos going on in the universe, and yet there is an amazing coherence or synergy between the celestial bodies, each doing what it was created to do.

God was ready to deal with my chaos; I just had to remember this was all about *divine* purpose. I am a small part of God's overall purpose in an unfolding universe. That insight brought down the walls of anxiety I felt within. Little by little they began to crack.

Listening to the echoing sounds
of the emotional deep

Hollowness can be rich if we learn how to listen to the harmony of the echoing sounds of the deep. I called deep into my soul, and an echo returned to affirm that I was still alive. Like Lazarus, I got ready to take my first steps out of the tomb of human anxiety. I wasn't doing anybody a good turn by pondering on my personal misery; the point was to learn.

I've come to call it *metanoia thinking*. *Metanoia* is about shifting paradigms; creating openness in one's spirit to accommodate and explore new and deeper discoveries of the heart and mind. If we don't think differently, better and higher in the pigsty of human existence, we will end up eating with pigs.

Metanoia is thinking for change in a way that reveals the hidden spots of a situation. It stands above and within the circumstances to obtain a sensitive and fuller perspective of the situation; and then moves on to make informed decisions about new and sustainable directions. Much like the African meerkat who stands on two legs to spy out the surroundings above the tall grass that covers him, and then scuttles for cover if there is any danger.

Metanoia is revolutionary because it turns traditional thinking upside down; it is evolutionary because it is an unfolding process of new thinking patterns, and transcendent because it has a built-in capacity to stand above itself in constructive judgement or self-criticism.

Metanoia is the shifting sands that blow the lid off the boiling pot of personal pain and experience and allow the creative steam in us to escape and to generate the clouds that bless us with fresh rain after a devastating drought. It's a renaissance of the human spirit to greater and beyond life possibilities, and a determination to pursue those possibilities in the context of God's purpose for our lives.

Purpose is not about who you are now; it's about who you are becoming in relation to the unfolding universe, and within God's greater purpose. We hardly ever realise that we are part of a great evolution and expansion of the universe because we are caught up in our little self-centred games on earth. We are very numb to the fact that we are part of an immense picture—a universal picture of many complexities and intricacies.

The *Matthew 6:33 imperative* is a challenge for us to seek first the Kingdom of God, but it doesn't promise that we will find what we are seeking. The challenge is to begin the journey, and as you travel along, the kingdom is given to you, and what you are given you must return to the earth and all who live in it.

Coming alive!

God ordered everything in its place for a purpose; true meaning is a discovery of self in the context of that purpose. As Mary Daly wrote (Clinebell, 1975:37): *"When I am coming alive I know that I am coming alive. The cosmic covenant means coming into a living harmony with the self, the universe, and God."*

No situation is hopeless enough for God. Ezekiel's prophecy in the valley of dry bones (Chap 37:1-14) is a tremendous inspiration for me. It is God's promise to Israel for restoration and deliverance. The prophet observed a message of hope against hope in a beyond-hopeless situation. Dry bones coming alive!

The image of a crucified Christ is completed only by the image of a resurrected and exalted Christ. When I hit rock bottom, the only other way available was the way up—I could not go further than I had already come. I had to see things differently, and on a higher level. My problems could not be solved on the same level on which they were created.

When we begin the journey back to where the Kingdom calls, we often have to cover the same distance as when we walked away. In some ways, we walk past familiar territory, but it's a different place because perspectives are changing. It's the only way we can identify the thorns and thistles that will make us never walk down that road again. It is the same sun shining, but it is a brand new day. We walk back to where we started, and it is a brand new place.

Life's rare gifts are never discovered on a treasure hunt on a distant island, they are right under your nose. Jesus said, *"The kingdom of God is within you."* As we travel back to where destiny calls, step by meticulous step we must heed Frankl's vital advice (1984:175): *"Live as if you were living for the second time and had acted the first time, as you are about to act now."*

I mentioned earlier that we do not choose to die; it is determined for us within God's greater scheme of things. For some it comes earlier, for others later, but eventually, it must come. It is unfortunate that we fear the inevitable and the ultimate, which seems to suggest that we have the cart before the horse, and half the time the wheels are coming off.

We do more to help the human body to survive above the grave, instead of helping the person to have a meaningful life. We worry about death instead of life, and in the process we lose the very life we are trying to preserve. When I tiptoed on the edges of death, I looked back; I didn't see much, except a crumbled kingdom I'd tried to build. I would have died with a sad song in my heart, "Nothing in my hands I bring, simply to the dross I cling."

The thought of dying empty literally scared the hell out of me. I wasn't afraid to die anymore; instead I developed a deeper passion for life. I lived to tell the tale, not only for my generation, but many more beyond. When my body is long in the grave, the irreplaceable word will still be making its rounds.

I had a dream the other day. Walking down the road I sang a song, and I was soon joined by one person, and another, and another; and before I knew it there was a tremendous crowd behind me singing the same song—faces I couldn't see, but whose voices I heard. A still small voice said to me, "Some of the people who are going to run with this song, you will never even get to see, or know."

Digging up our own skeletons is a painful process, but it is loaded with the possibility of new beginnings. As much as the past can be liberating, it can be trapping too. Revisiting our past is intended to unleash a learning process, enabling us not to repeat past mistakes. Skeletons belong to the grave, not the closet; when they have no further use for the future, we must bury them. The prophet said, *Isa 43:18* *"Forget the former things; do not dwell on the past."*

2

BUILDING A NEW IDENTITY

Ephesians 1:11-12(The Message) *"It's in Christ that we find out who we are and what we are living for. Long before we first heard of Christ and got our hopes up, he had his eye on us, had designs on us for glorious living, part of the overall purpose he is working out in everything and everyone."*

The process in *metanoia thinking* begins with *learning:* as the saying goes, "learn from your mistakes". The other dimension is reconstructing the image base in your subconscious. You can't move forward with images of the past still in your mind; what you remove must be replaced by other, more authentic and powerful images—images that reconnect you to God, the earth and the universe.

IDENTITY IS A BIG THING IN AFRICA

When I grew up, my father was not around; he and my mother were never married—and that was all too common in the black townships around South Africa. I grew up using my mother's last name, with very scanty knowledge of who my father was. My struggle with identity began that early.

When I got to know for sure who my father was, he wasn't using his real last name. He was an "illegal" immigrant from Zimbabwe who came searching for work in South Africa; changing last names was common among work-seekers from neighbouring countries—it made blending into society quicker and easier. Apartheid was unkind to its own, not to mention foreigners, even though they filled the gold mines to the brim. In his adventures, he ran into a lawyer who was willing to lend him his last name; the man arranged for an identity document with the name Shabalala instead of Maphosa.

My crisis got deeper; I couldn't use his last name, let alone a borrowed one; so I settled for my mother's last name. For a long time, my mother's family was the only family I knew, but the quest to know my father's family never subsided—in Africa, identity is always associated with your father's side of the family.

There is no such thing as an illegitimate child!

One of my greatest frustrations was growing up as a so-called illegitimate child. One day my mother brought along the new man in her life, and it sparked a seed of hope in me. I walked up to him one afternoon with homework in my hands, and I was simply dismissed with a cold and stern look of disapproval, as if to say, "Don't ever try that again." My spirit sank. I found out later that the man couldn't read or write.

That's how it works with promises; you just don't walk up and claim promises in wrong places. In God's mercy and love, no one is more legitimate than the other; we all have the right to approach the throne of grace through our Lord Jesus Christ. We can assert with confidence, "I can boldly approach the throne of God because I am a child of God." In Christ, every child has the right to be born!

The premise of prayer is the legitimate promise of the son/daughter relationship we have with God. So we, ^{Hebrews 4:16}"come boldly to the throne of our gracious God. There we will receive his mercy, and find grace to help us when we need it most". Children can be selfish, and in their ignorance, arrogance and innocence they can say some painful things. I walked up to a crowd of children a while ago, and they were gloating about their fathers' achievements. One who was particularly boastful was reminded, "He is not your father . . . you are only a step-child." As sons and daughters of God, we don't have to deal with that kind of coldness; we approach God's throne of grace with all confidence, and the legitimacy of our identity is made authentic only by faith in God through Christ our Lord.

WHO AM I?

Identity is a big thing; you have to know your roots, people say, however humble or classy. I didn't know mine, except for a brief visit to the then Rhodesia when I was about five years old. The only thing I remember about the trip is that on our return my father vanished. My maternal grandfather and uncles wanted to kill him because he left me and my mother back in Zimbabwe.

Nobody knew much about these strangers from other countries, and in those days, there were many unproven stories of cannibalism in neighbouring countries north of the Limpopo River. My maternal grandparents had no way of knowing whether we were alive, or in some stranger's belly. One of my uncles ran into my father in a local beer-hall; he could not account satisfactorily for our whereabouts; and the chase began . . . he never stopped running.

I have two older brothers from another father, but I couldn't fully identify with them either, and my crisis deepened. Throughout my young life I struggled with two issues, legitimacy, and identity. My brothers on my mother's side proved to be the only brothers I would ever have. I had two other brothers on my father's side, and they were dead. My sister on my father's side died of HIV/AIDS. In a real sense, I was on my own.

Being "illegitimate" meant you had no right to be born, unless your parents were married, and using your mother's last name suggested being abandoned by your father. As a little boy, I couldn't run to anyone for protection from bullies in the street; more often than not I was merely dismissed and sent back home crying. I had to learn to fight my own battles, and the emotional pain of not knowing where my father was grew unbearable.

"Azusa Street" comes to Africa

My mother took me to Somlandela church revivals at 4th Street and 4th Avenue in Etwatwa, Benoni Old Location. They had banners hanging all over the place, *"Jesus is the answer!"* Another read, *"Back To God!"* This was "312 Azusa Street" come to Africa: People were singing the Zulu version of the chorus:

> I will follow; I will follow Jesus
> Wherever he goes; I will follow

There was an undeniably charged atmosphere, something thick in the air that was turning everybody upside down and inside out. People called it the Holy Spirit, and others thought it was some form of unknown witchcraft. The commotion was unbelievable; people were praying loudly; grown men and women were crying, screaming, rolling and singing all at the same time—yet the chaos had a restraint I could not explain. An unquestionable moral revolution was taking place—something powerful was turning this whole place around. There were indisputable miraculous healings all over the place; and whatever this was, it was finding its way into my young heart.

I couldn't put into plain words whatever was happening, but it was obviously authentic. The people here were warm, loving and joyful; there was something different, but I couldn't put my finger on it. There were men, good looking, strong, always clean and nicely clad. I wanted to be like them when I grew up . . .

Rival hooligans came from every direction handing in their weapons of crime and receiving Christ as Saviour. It was a perfect scene straight out of Nicky Cruz's *The Cross and the Switchblade*. Etwatwa had its share of notorious gangsters, Mashalashala, Ma-Rooikamp, and many others patterned after gang life in African-American residential locations. In fact, some gangsters called themselves the Americans.

I started going to Sunday school, and one day our teacher caught me reading something out in English to a group of other children around me. He was so impressed, and his excitement stayed with me for a long time. By some inspiration I spoke and read English as my second language well from around the age of six or seven; it was uncommon in those days, and I came to be known as the "small English boy".

I didn't know why this teacher was so taken with me, but I just loved being appreciated by someone like him; it made me feel wanted, and in some small way I was starting to identify with the situation. He started arranging for me to read or recite long bible extracts in major church conferences; and my crowd of admirers grew. I saw more and more men I envied, and felt increasingly wanted.

These men were nothing like my father, or my uncles who were always under the influence of some intoxicating fatal concoction called *skop-donner*, or *imbamba*. In some instances the homemade brew would be made stronger by dipping a car battery into the concoction overnight—it gave it the "kick".

I had my own list of potential stepfathers that my mother didn't know about; and as the candidates got married one by one, my covert aspirations broke one piece at a time. If my wishes had turned into horses . . . but they never do.

WHEN WALLS COME CRUMBLING DOWN

In the early 1960s a full-force programme of removals was implemented under the apartheid system in African townships, and Etwatwa was relocated to Daveyton, another township on the other side of town. The House Church at 4th Street and 4th Avenue came crashing down. When we finally left Etwatwa, I felt like a piece of my soul was buried underneath the rubble—that began a hatred for apartheid that stayed with me for a long time.

We arrived at a house on 12903 Mashiane Street on a cold winter's afternoon; and everything was foreign—new people, neighbours, school and new church. I was back to square one in my crisis of identity. Daveyton was a lot cleaner compared to where we came from, but Etwatwa was all I knew. All the dirty water and shit we had stepped on in the street, or that ran down an exposed drain during rainy seasons was our shit. The stench of urine that hung all over the place was our stench, and we wanted to hang on to it.

In Etwatwa there had been some strange things going on, like the Sgodo family who seemed to suffer endless torments from a form of madness they could not exorcise. For instance, New Year's Eve was most exciting because we had a way of annoying drunken adults who were unkind to children. The township had the notorious bucket system for sanitation—and we took buckets full of human excrement and threw them against the victim's door. One of us would throw a firecracker into the house to scare the people out, and when anyone opened the door, the bucketful would just pour into the doorway—and we ran for dear life . . .

The new place was different, sanitation was more sophisticated; we pulled a chain and everything disappeared, we didn't know where. We had to find new ways of excitement. They were nothing like the ridiculous games we had played; some older boys almost crushed my skull with a big rock thrown from a tree as I passed directly below. On one occasion, a bully threw my male cousin into thorny bushes—just to get him scratched.

My father was still hidden somewhere between the truckloads that brought people into the new township. I had no way of knowing where he was, until he surfaced long after we had settled in the strange land. It didn't matter, he was still a stranger; those occasional drop-by's were nothing unusual, they came once in a while with long stretches in between. I struggled to identify with him.

The new church wasn't exciting; the people knew me, but they didn't give me the attention I had received at 4th Street and 4th Avenue. Sunday school was different, and sooner rather than later, I stopped going. Everyone had their own reasons for staying away; but largely, it was because this wasn't what we knew back where we came from. We were sulking; the House Church was buried, but it lived on in our hearts.

UKHEHLA: THE OLD MAN

The Rev. Nicholas Bhengu was the champion of the spiritual revival that was sweeping parts of the country in those days, and at 4th Street and 4th Avenue everybody spoke about "The old man", or "*Ukhehla*". To many people, he was the closest thing to God on earth after Christ and the apostles.

I got my first break to see him in a conference in Orlando, Soweto, in the early 60's. I was always this little inquisitive kid who kept sneaking his way between adults to see the things that caught my attention. There he was, right before my eyes, our father, and everyone called him "Ubaba." He had been abroad for some time, and everybody wanted to see what he looked like. Coming from America in those days was like returning from Mars. I curiously wanted to see what this creature from outer space looked like. There was something different about him, but he wasn't from Mars. He didn't send people away with bellies full of sand, he filled them with God; and they blessed him with every conceivable desire of the heart one could imagine

Ukhehla spoke of his evangelistic adventures in some faraway country called the United States of America; he mentioned how he was preaching on the south side of Chicago and hundreds of black people responded to his captivating and thunderous altar call. Always in a black suit and wearing a bow tie, he was the tall powerful sight no one could miss.

He commanded everyone's respect, and in those early days, he drove around in a brand-new German car; a luxury most black business people could not afford and every bit of it was a gift from people whose lives he touched with the Gospel of Christ. He would shout one "Hallelujah," and the whole house would go "spiritually" berserk!

The next time I caught a glimpse of the old man was in a little township east of Johannesburg. I was twenty-one years old, just a few months after I had made a serious and informed commitment to Christ. He still had the same spiritual aura I had heard about and witnessed so much as a child; and I wanted to be like him.

I saw him again for the third time, almost a year later, this time in Zimbabwe. I was there searching for my long-lost aunt who had left South Africa two years before I was born. Ukhehla was outside his usual terrain, but the aura still prevailed. People jammed the auditorium where he was to speak; he tried to get them to come back some other time because he was very tired. The audience refused to budge; many had travelled long distances just to see and hear him. He spoke, but his fatigue showed throughout. I still wanted to be like him; if anything, I was going to be "the old man" of my generation. My calling into the ministry was sealed.

Ukhehla was a distant yet strong positive part of the forces that influenced my early childhood. I never met him face-to-face, I was too young for that, and he was too far removed to give an audience to children. If I did meet him, I probably would have collapsed—his presence had a magical effect about it. There was usually a stampede of people who wanted to bask in the aura of his company, and then go back to mimic his hoarse "Hallelujah" voice and warrior gesticulations.

Southern Africa School of "Eulogy"

By the time I reported for Bible School, I was still swinging like a pendulum between many dizzying identity extremes, still searching for who I was. I was hopeful—I'd seen many people come from Bible School and be as powerful as I wanted to be. In these new surroundings, I ran into some old faces I remembered from when I was a child in

Sunday school—the 4th Street and 4th Avenue identity was starting to form again.

One man had become the undisputed national superintendent of the church, and another was a popular bible teacher. They were at the forefront of a completely new movement started years earlier from a split with the mother body. They knew me personally, and I decided to join their ranks. I admired them a lot, now I was one of them; and that sent my ego spiralling out of control. Finally, I could prefix my name with the title of "Reverend". They spoke my kind of English, so I wasn't totally lost from my earlier beginnings. Some light was beginning show in the dark tunnel of my identity crisis.

Bible School was good for many reasons; new friendships began to form, and I became part of an elite group called the Revival Team. The team travelled to different churches around the country to assist in evangelistic campaigns, and to promote the school in its drive for new students. In some sense it increased our network of influence; we became known, people invited us to their weddings, we became "accredited" preachers and interpreters; and that popularity gave me an identity boost I needed badly—I was being appreciated by people who made more sense about a lot of things. The eulogy made more sense than the theology.

It seemed like my identity struggles were dissolving, but one thing was still missing—I was not married. Marriage was a major obstacle for any soon-to-be Rev. My identity woes began to unfold in a deeper way, just when I thought they were going away. As it turned out, marriage would inflict a lasting and deep dent on the image and identity I was trying so hard to build.

MUCH ADO ABOUT "I DO"

Bible School had a rule # 7. It was intended to regulate relations between men and women on campus, but somehow students found their way around it. Everybody at Bible School wanted to get married; it was a very exciting topic among both men and women. Many met their future spouse in the quiet corridors of the classroom, the library, the kitchen, or the chapel itself, but it had to be hush-hush. Nevertheless, even the faculty broke its own rules by arranging for some students to marry others; if you were lucky, they would even pay your dowry.

I met someone from the crowd I arrived with in our first year, and we later broke the news to our pastor that we were seeing each other. We were never married, though. I tried another relationship, it too fell through. When I finally I got married, I'd been through three failed relationships—and the trend was set . . .

My first wife was just finishing high school when we started preparing for marriage, and I was in the final year of Bible School—perfect timing. I was very quick to replace one relationship with another; the thought of going into ministry without a wife was just unimaginable, and everything else around me was saying, "Hurry-hurry!" That "hurry-hurry" thing was intended to protect us from "falling" into sin. For most people that was the chief objective; sexual sin was the highest expression of the unpardonable.

Our marriage was a disaster from the beginning; my wife had her own ideas about many things, and so did I. She was struggling with her own issues of identity, and we couldn't meet each other halfway—even worse, we didn't know how. Nothing had prepared us for this; not home, not church—nothing! Two total strangers had come together, and the pastor who married us proudly announced, "Now you can fire up, my son!" With that, we were granted permission for sex—marriage was sex, not relationship—and the drift was all too common.

Nothing was out in the open in a "hush-hush/hurry-hurry" world. One scene I could never forget kept flashing before me. I remembered how I walked into a pastor's home and his wife was swearing and cursing the man of God. Yet, these two were "dear-ing" and "sweet-ing" each other in public, everything else in private was hush-hush. This "one flesh" was obviously divided in private, but did a good job in public relation stunts.

Nobody had ever told me there are two sides to every coin—as far as most of us could tell, marriage was heaven on earth, and the hell took me by total surprise. My own situation got worse, and I just didn't know what to do. Cracks began to show in this new identity I was trying to build, and soon the whole thing came crashing down—ten long years of pain and strain were flushed down the drain. An important vestige of my identity adventures was broken, and by the time the marriage ended, I was faceless.

Things were happening that I couldn't talk to anybody about. In some cases people knew more about my marriage than I did; their faces told hidden but sorry stories. With a broken marriage behind me, keeping an authentic "ministry-image" seemed impossible. "Divorce" was taboo for anyone; how much more "A man of God." What is the first thing I would say about marriage when my own was in shreds; especially in an environment that had no room for human error?

People started looking at me like a piece of filth the dog had just dragged in. Piercing and unforgiving gossip flew around; and vultures from miles around caught the stench of my dead flesh. And with every landing, they gouged my eyes out, and ripped my flesh to the bone. The situation had its own hyenas, friends and foes tore chunks of me to ravage; hidden by the shadows of a starless night. I was thrown into the dark abyss of a system I helped uphold. I looked around for my earlier role models; they too drowned in the same waters.

My second marriage came shortly after my first one ended, and wrapped in the new package was an opportunity to get away from all the noise that surrounded me. I was willing to give myself another chance, and I ventured into the corporate world.

I didn't like my new world at all; pasted smiles, bootlicking, endless hours keeping minutes—here, the business of business was business, not creating personal identity. The "three musketeer" mind-set was all too prevalent: *"Every one for himself, and God for us all."*

That was a culture shock; I'd been in the corporate world before, but only for brief stints. My mind-set was shifted from being something

I didn't know what to putting food on the table. For more than ten years I had heard people talk about that, and a rosy pension at the end of one's working life—maybe buying a farm somewhere, playing golf, or going fishing. Was that all?

Deep inside me, I knew there was more, I didn't know what it was, or at least I pretended not to know—so I decided to blend in with the crowd. After all, corporate identity is what matters for many people. If I worked my way up the ladder, maybe my picture would get to appear in the "People on the move" column of some popular glossy magazine—that would help boost my shattered identity.

It didn't matter if the ladder stood against the right wall or not; I had to put food on the table. That story also ended on a bitter note—thirty years later, I was still struggling with my identity—and tongue-hanging dog-tired. If I was going to give it another shot, it had to be a lifetime lasting one; I didn't have another thirty years.

WHOSE AM I?

When I read Warren's book (2002:17), the very first sentence hit me between the eyes, *"It's not about you."* Why was I gasping for breath so bad, when life wasn't even about me? Why was I so anxious about something I didn't create? This whole thing should have been about God from the very beginning—every detail of it.

Warren wasn't saying anything I didn't know, but it was coming through with a newness that confounded everything I knew about anything. If life wasn't about me, what was I doing here living it? That wasn't a suicidal question; I just had to figure out very deeply my reason for being.

Paul let the Ephesians in on the secret, ^{Ephesians 1:11-12 (The Message)} *"It's in Christ that we find out who we are and what we are living for. Long before we first heard of Christ and got our hopes up, he had his eye on us, had designs on us for glorious living, part of the overall purpose he is working out in everything and everyone."*

That scripture answered many questions for me, among others, and my identity crisis was resolved. In a deeper sense, I began to see myself in relation to God and God's overall purpose for the universe. My parents were only agents, not architects, of my destiny; my identity begins and ends with God.

BUILDING NEW IMAGES OF THE SUBCONSCIOUS

The mind thinks in picture-forms. That assertion came as fresh rain on dry land, especially as I gradually discovered how picturesque biblical scripture is. The prophets conveyed their messages in vivid images, the psalmists chanted their songs of praise in metaphors, Christ taught in parables, and the book of Revelation depicts the end times in imagery.

As I began the process of unlearning the old, I replaced each picture with a new biblical image—one peel-off at a time. This was more than a psychological process; it was the beginning of a fresh walk with God. What I did now felt like I'd never done before. Like Nicodemus covered by the dark night, I felt a new thing emerge into the *Light*. I was born again.

All my life I wanted to touch, see, smell, taste and hear the sound of cowhide drums rumble my name into the echelons of human prestige. It felt good when it happened to some extent, but when it was taken away, my very soul was demanded of me. Then, I asked Eric Fromm's question, *"If I am what I have, and what I have is lost; who then am I?"* My identity bearings began to shift: "Whose I am" began to answer the perennial question of human existence: "Who am I?"

I am who "I AM" says I am

(© Steve Mochechane)

I am created in the image of God.
I stand within and above God's creation.
In Christ I return to a state of divine wholeness
I am not defined by will, heredity, or environment
I recognise that these are not permanent.
I am who **"I AM"** says I am

In Christ, I am blessed with permanent blessings in the heavenly realm
I may be in this world, but I am not of the world
Therefore, the world cannot define or limit, who I can become in God.
Through Christ, I am who **"I AM"** says I am

Nothing is more powerful than who I am created to be
That place in the universe kept only for me
In me, God returns to bless the earth
With God, nothing is impossible.

3

YOU ARE THE ONLY ONE OF YOUR KIND

Everyone should be respected as an individual,
but no one should be idolised.

Albert Einstein.

"Fit in, or ship out" is a very popular cliché in the corporate world: you either join the culture and politics of the situation, or you are out. That is a very common trend in any group; in our quest for approval we spend most of our time not actualising personal passion and potential, but trying to measure up to the expectations of others—feeling under—or over-utilised.

One of the things you discover during the process of identity reconstruction is that no two people are the same—even conjoined twins. While others may not be totally comfortable with the person you are becoming, you have to land in it with both feet firmly on the ground. Fake does not save face, you have to stick with who you are and actualise your uniqueness to bless, not curse.

The Kingdom journey is a form of spiritual metamorphosis—an evolution into becoming the butterfly that each one of us was created to be, and every butterfly must fly its own unique flight.

"A MONGREL AMONG THOROUGHBREDS"

For most of my life in the ministry, I've been what Reinhold Niebuhr called *a mongrel among thoroughbreds.* I've always been off tangent from what others are doing, or saying. I was too questioning, too political, too much of this, too little of that—the list of accusations and labels was infinite.

Thinking of politics, my heart was never really into it, but my hatred for apartheid was deep. Not only was it stripping off whatever little racial identity we had, it was killing us. During the so-called Soweto Uprising in 1976, I missed death by a few inches, and ten years later, I was literally picking up and burying dead bodies of children massacred by a merciless political system.

I saw terrified women braving the deadly streets looking for their wounded or dead children—someone had to walk with them down that Jericho Road. For most pastors, passing by on the other side was a safe bet. Pastors in the fundamental fraternity started avoiding me like a plague; especially when I opposed support for one of us who was also one of them.

The reverend in question was a police officer often seen in questionable police activity in the township; in one report in the media he lied about the death of a young boy shot by the security forces; and that didn't sit well with the "Young Lions"—they went on an uncontrollable rampage to burn down his house. Reverends were on both sides of the divide; some played Dr Jekyll and Mr Hyde so well that they lost face with the community. I was too much in the open for comfort.

I had become too different; I even wore a clerical collar. Apartheid was vicious, but it did have some respect for men of the cloth; and in the thick of smoke and gunfire, you had to be clearly identified—it was a matter of life and death.

In those days, nobody wanted to be seen on the wrong side of apartheid. Anything could happen, including being roasted alive in a remote camping site northwest of Johannesburg while the chefs shared a beer to celebrate the sound of your exploding body. I was endangering people's comfort zones, and nobody wanted to be seen around me.

One early morning the security forces knocked on my door, and they ransacked our house from top to bottom. My wife was terrified, and our baby boy hung onto me crying as apartheid agents took me away. They staged a real show outside, with military trucks lined up and down the street, and members of the defence force surrounding our house. They found nothing on me, except that I hid some student ringleaders in a remote village in what was then Bophuthatswana—I paid dearly for it.

While in detention a white police officer walked in on me while I was reading the bible, and he thought it was a joke; little did he realise how much inspiration I drew from it in that God-forsaken place. His instrument of oppression was my source of liberation.

In prison we prayed, and played some religious games on the prison warders. Whenever there was something serious to discuss, we gathered around lunchtime, and pretended to have a prayer meeting. I would facilitate the meeting with a bible in my hand, and chant some amens, and the meeting would go on in a language the white warders didn't understand. We got away with it every time.

After my second detention, I "walked" into a scholarship through the Educational Opportunities Council in Johannesburg to pursue graduate studies in Evanston, Illinois. The two-year break was more than welcome, especially from a first marriage that turned me purple with frustration and a Christian community that saw wrong in everything I did.

WELCOME TO AMERICA!

Garret Evangelical Theological Seminary at Northwestern University was a breath of much-needed fresh air. I just couldn't miss the opportunity, so I left South Africa in the early hours of the morning—the last time I checked, apartheid could stop the trip. Once, I missed a Billy Graham all-expenses-paid trip to Singapore because I was in detention. I sat in a prison cell eating my heart out as fellow participants were bidding relatives goodbye on a local radio station. For the most part, it was a first one couldn't afford to miss—going abroad was a big deal!

I landed in the US in the autumn of my first year of study; two weeks earlier than required because I wanted to adjust—this was my first trip abroad. Evanston was spooky quiet because most people were out of town. I wondered how many students there were with a campus stretching three-quarters of town—"This is a University town," someone said, "that's why it's so quiet."

My first culture shock happened on the first Sunday—the woman who fetched me from the airport invited me to her highly recommended church. She and her husband were the only ones who knew I was alive in a strange land. They even offered me my first international call; and back home, my son was beginning the long wait for my uncertain return.

We walked into a small United Methodist church on Maple Avenue, and the first thing that jumped out at me was that the seating arrangement was different—people sat face to face instead of in rows. The dress code was very informal, and the pastor was a woman who looked like a man in a dress—it was an "inclusive church". Gays and lesbians were welcome here.

Picking up the absolute shock on my face, a "queer"-looking man gave me a hearty long and warm squeeze, "Welcome to America!" I was breathing heavily, and that hug kept me on my feet—the fundamental in me was on the verge of collapse. I was "tangent" and all that, but this was something else; and it was just the beginning . . .

When school started, it was policy to use "inclusive language"—using male pronouns for God was absolute taboo. "God is spirit, and spirit has no gender" the argument went. "If God is a man, how do women identify with him?" "Our Father" in the Lord's Prayer became "Our God", which accommodated both men and women. The whole thing left me feeling very dizzy—back home, this was not even a subject under consideration—not until twenty years later.

Discrimination of other students based on gender or sexual orientation was strictly prohibited—and the school had its large share of gay/lesbian students. They were not there for fun; they were preparing for ministry in one of the many denominations represented across the student body. There were all shades of evangelicals, fundamentals, Roman Catholics, Episcopalian, and a wide range of international students. I was getting dizzier with every day that passed by.

I thought I was open-minded, but this was closing down my thinking all together—now, I was the "thoroughbred among mongrels". Class discussions ranged from anything to everything—the nuclear arms race, feminism, education, racial/sexual discrimination, abortion, drugs in South America, euthanasia, sanctions, Christian socialism. With South Africa hot on international racial controversies, I became an unauthorised centre of attraction—people touched and hugged me, just to feel a live black South African.

It was fascinating, yet it was scary—this community was nothing like I'd known over the years. They were even more questioning than I was; they even asked God questions. In fundamental circles and cycles, that was way off base.

There was mention of God, and in this new context, people were willing to let their minds go. There were no doctrinal overseers here; everybody was obsessed with inquiry, and in many cases, a genuine desire to know God more.

My theological background was straight and narrow; you could never ask a question without feeling like a little devil among angels;

you always had to move within "approved" doctrinal perimeters. Here, you didn't have to be "one of us" to be accepted.

I sat in Rosemary Ruether's *"Sexism and God"* talk and for the first time, I saw women from a perspective of strength; not the "weaker vessels" overstretched so much by fundamental theology. She was deeply spiritual and thoroughly intellectual; in my background, the two did not reconcile—in most cases you had to surrender your brain with every altar call.

I became a member of the Program of African Studies at Northwestern University; before then Africa was as foreign as Nelson Mandela was—most of us knew more about Napoleon Bonaparte than we did about Patrice Lumumba. The program hosted African scholars from everywhere, and had the largest Africana library in the world—was that manna from heaven or what?

Among my firsts, I met South Africans in exile—and these "aliens" were like me, they spoke my language and laughed at the same jokes. Apartheid painted a different picture of the exiles—poor, hungry, stranded in the bush and walking around with bare behinds. These were decent people, some were highly qualified and respected in the world—and they desperately wanted to go back home.

Reading a banned book in a free world was like floating in the air without a parachute, and yet landing safely. Apartheid had a tendency to ban every piece of literature it found offensive. When I saw Mandela's picture for the first time, I was almost booked into a mental asylum—the excitement was just indescribable. In 1988, the thought of a free Mandela was as far as north is from south.

Like everybody else, I was hoping against hope for his freedom—maybe in my lifetime—if I was lucky. I was lucky. When Mandela was released in early 1990, South Africans in Chicago partied like it was never going to end. We played South African music all night—the same music we despised on home soil. We became overnight celebrities on television all over Chicago-land—freedom was closer than we thought.

I lived for two years in that Northwestern/Garret environment, and by the time I finished school I was smoking. I was alone in a foreign land; nothing was even close to the things I knew and was beginning to miss so much. One day I walked into a little shop in Evanston, and out of the corner of my eye, I caught sight of "Rothmans"—a South African cigarette brand name! I bought a box as a souvenir to put up in a corner somewhere in my dormitory—just to remind me of home, and soon picked up a habit that sent me off on a fundamental tangent.

This was Garret Evangelical, and salvation in Christ didn't rest on a cigarette stub—here God was a journey—a very long journey. My new habit was not turning heads at all, everybody went on with their own spiritual struggles; back home it would have become a "rumble in the jungle".

These evangelicals were not "speaking in tongues", but most of them had a spiritual depth I admired, and they came in various packages. A woman professor, Marty Scott, took us on a train ride to Cabrini Green on the south side of Chicago with one question in mind, "If Christ rode with us on this trip, what do you think his reaction would be?", or "If Christ lived in Cabrini Green, what would he do?" This could have been another township in South Africa—and for the first time I could relate Christ to my own suffering.

Riding the L-train from Evanston to the south side of Chicago was an experience of a lifetime. The north and the south were very different—the north somewhat cleaner, predominantly white and more educated. The south—dirtier, predominantly black and less educated—for a while it felt like Johannesburg. "Brothers" stood at a street corner throwing dice; there were liquor stores on every twist and turn, dilapidated and burnt down buildings; drugs, drugs and more drugs; every open space had a broken down vehicle. Every other window in the black-occupied "projects" showed signs of smoke; I thought I was going to hear someone say "Voetsek!"[2]

There are many things about the fundamental tradition that remain part of me, but in that situation, I was shedding much of what I'd always known how to do. Among other things, my pastoral model was changing—as a pastor in my church, I was ordained to find the lost, traumatise the found, marry the unprepared, anathematise the divorced, and bury the dead. My Sunday sermon was a well-crafted dreamy address with no implications for human experience at all—it's what I was paid to do—if I was paid at all.

My return to the land of sworn hypocrisy

I've always been fascinated by Rabbi Nicodemus's night-covered visit to Christ; it represents the way we would often do things in the pastoral fraternity. When I landed in Johannesburg just three days after my graduation, a part of my heart sank. I knew I was back in the land of sworn secrecy—or hypocrisy. My newfound face would not be recognised at all, so I put on the face that everyone knew before I left for America. I felt like a lowered yo-yo wrapped around a finger that desperately wanted to lift me up.

Had it not been for the angst I felt in my son's voice the Friday before, I would have stayed on, and perhaps even explored opportunities for further study. Disappearing abroad was a common trend in South Africa, especially if you had some tiffs with apartheid. While abroad, I met people who had been away from home for many years; many were on self-imposed exile. Back home people were filling my son with stories that I wasn't coming back—that started me packing. I was so worried that I left many things behind, especially books that I knew were rarer than a needle in a haystack in South Africa.

---

[2]   "Voetsek" is a common swearword in South African townships; used particularly to scare away dogs. If you hear it anywhere else in the world, the person is South African, or once visited the country. In a foreign land, you get to appreciate anything that is home-grown.

Something about my thinking had shifted radically, and part of me was getting seriously bored with the usual fundamental routine of hush-hushes, and hide-and-seek behaviours. Why would one hide from people what God can see? With an attitude like that, I ran millimetres short of being branded a heretic. In the measure of some, I was completely beyond redemption, not even the grace of God was sufficient for me.

THE KEY IS EXPLORING DIVERSITY, NOT ENCOURAGING UNIFORMITY

We like being among people who think and do things like we do, because it is easier to be unified if we stand on common ground, and yet that is more of a myth than reality; people will always have their differences—large or small.

"The myth of uniformity is responsible for more cruelty than we care to think about; from family disputes to international disputes. Everybody encourages exploring what we have in common, only for the simmering differences to blow up in our face. That is how Julius Caesar got to be murdered by his closest friends."

"Diversity does not demand surrender. It creates an environment in which our differences can be explored." Because if we don't do that, even what we have in common will be lost. Uniformity stifles, while diversity encourages growth, even if the stones have to rough up on each other a bit—it's the only way to be smooth. Of course, it is easier said than done. The pain that comes with exploring diversity is what makes it so difficult to deal with—yet it is indispensable pain.

BREAK YOUR FALLOW GROUND!

I was a direct product of an intense programme of religious teachings that refused to be probed for relevance, genuineness and sincerity. I was strong on compliance to human structures, and wanting on commitment to God through Christ. That attitude trapped me in the confines of a self-imposed religious rigidity—a prisoner of my own system.

Often in our desire to appease God, we develop systems and rituals that negate the very things we desire. We lose sight of the overarching purpose of why we do what we do, because it is all lost in the attempt to protect what we cherish—in the process we lose the very thing we want to protect.

My problem was not with all the things I tried to do to find meaning, or identity; it was my relation to them—I wanted to know how situations could benefit me and not how I could add value to them. We all know President Kennedy's famous statement, *"Ask not what America can do for you; but what you can do for America"*. It is only when you do something for America that America can do something for you—that principle took a while to sink in.

For much of the time I stood in reaction to situations, when I should have been proactive—giving back to life what it had given to me. Life had given to me the gift of life itself—how was I returning the investment? That was a sobering thought; for a long time, I asked the question, "What's in it for me?" If I couldn't figure out the benefits, I simply walked out.

I spent so much time walking out; I ended up with the very nothing I feared. I sat in a dark corner wondering if there was not more to life than the things that were blown away like chaff driven by a desert wind. Was there nothing more enduring?

When my fallow ground started breaking up, something else opened up—nothing is more enduring than God is. I knew that as knowledge, not experience, and I discovered that real life is more experience than knowledge. Some people have knowledge without experience, but very few have experience without knowledge—experience still proves to be the best teacher.

Nicodemus knew about God, but his experience was wanting—that is a very bitter pill to swallow, especially when you think you are tenured in what you do. I thought I knew God, and yet I had not even begun to scratch the surface. For the most part, I embraced the devil as an angel of light.

WE ARE SPIRITUAL BEINGS WITH A HUMAN EXPERIENCE

My biggest challenge was to redefine my spirit relation with God. Everything else I tried drew empty: church, people, family, friends—I couldn't go on embracing what I didn't know, especially because most things fell apart just when I had surrendered my all. Only one thing remained—God.

I had to try God again; there was something about my first attempt that didn't feel right—something more human than spirit. I started right, but somewhere along the way, I switched spirit authenticity for human endorsement. I was fine, for just as long as I measured up to my own or another's expectation.

I had my own checklist of things to become, which was not always compatible with other people's checklist of things I would never become. Both were measured on some ephemeral standard that had me running for years. There was a third list emerging, things that I am by faith in the Christ of God; I just had to believe and receive the grace and mercy of God. In my heart, a melody rang:

> Mercy there was great; and grace was free
> Pardon there was multiplied to me
> There my burdened soul found liberty
> At Calvary!

Nothing was new; there was just a blockage in the process. We had one like that in the sewage system on our farm; the draining reservoir was blocked and water was not running through; everything we tried to get through came right back. A big tree had grown roots into the passageway—we dug, and chopped, and dug again; and as soon as the roots were removed, the waters started flowing again. It brought tremendous relief. Discovering who you really are in God gives you a fresh start—breathing your own breath again.

It's not easy being your own person in a "copier" world where everybody wants to be like everyone else. We get sucked in because we are all sold out on the mad rush to worship idols of our environment. We rush for the wide gate, and in the process, many are crushed in the stampede. The narrow gate is a one person at a time, never to be repeated experience.

When I finally decided to settle with who I was in God, a whole new world opened up before me; there was so much to cover, a lifetime was simply not enough. In the corporate world, I looked forward to something called retirement; I didn't have the faintest clue what I was going to do with my life after that.

4

THE POWER OF PERSONAL VISION

Matthew 7: 13-14 (NLT) *"You can enter God's Kingdom only through the narrow gate. The highway to hell is broad, and the gate is wide for the many who choose that way. But the gateway to life is very narrow and the road is difficult, and only a few find it"*

J esus spoke of the narrow gate, and how few are they who find it. Biblical scripture does not pretend that finding one's gift is easy; neither does it say that a gift is some little one-time wrapped up package stashed away under a Christmas tree somewhere. Unearthing the Kingdom within us is a journey; we are exposed to new gifts on every level in a lifelong dynamic pilgrimage of novel discoveries.

The wide gate syndrome is prevalent because it is popular—doing what everybody else is doing, and the winner takes all. The challenge is to win, not to actualise, and once we bow to that idol, the highway to hell opens up even broader. We must win whatever the cost.

I grew up wanting to be like someone else, when was I going to be what God created me to become. In the environment that raised me, that thinking was non-existent, you could never become more than what your surroundings dictated—unless by the grace of God you managed to transcend the prevailing attitude.

The narrow gate mentality is not being narrow minded. By contrast, it is leveraging your search on what is really meaningful to you, and then focusing every ounce of strength in the achievement of that one thing. Paul wrote to the Philippians, ^{Phil 3:13} *"Brothers, I do not consider myself yet to have taken hold of it. But one thing I do: Forgetting what is behind and straining toward what is ahead."*

Personal vision involves strain, that's why it must be something you are passionate about almost to the point of obsession. If you know what to die for, then, and only then, do you know what to live for. You are going to die anyway, so you might as well make your living worth the while.

The human body is an amazing piece of work—seeing eyes, hearing ears, tasting tongue—every single thread has a special and specific function to fulfil. Some parts are small, and some are big, yet no function is too small to perform. Every part matters, and the whole is as effective as the sum of its parts.

When things fall apart, the first question that comes to mind is, "Do I still matter?" We ask that question in relation to the environmental things that used to define us, and when they are taken away, a bottomless void opens up under our feet. We are reduced to a shadow of our former selves—or so we think. The problem is not what we lost, but how we think in relation to what we lost.

When I got to that point, a still small voice said, "You still have you." I knew I was not a pig—so what was I doing in the sty? I had no excuse to be there. I could only understand that when I started to see myself in relation to God. I am created in the image of God, but the bad voice said, "You lost it!" The good one responded, "Jesus died to restore it!" For as long as you breathe another breath, there is no reason in the universe to stay down.

Not everyone needs to go through a pigsty moment to come to their senses—but it has a sobering effect. You start looking for depth and meaning in rare places, because you can't afford the same mistake twice. Pigsty moments send you on a deep dive into the coral reef of your innermost being to discover and retrieve what you didn't even know existed. Rare gifts don't lie on the surface, but when they finally emerge, the very people who questioned your sanity return to applaud your achievements—even better, they want to be part of the process.

PRAYER IS HOW WE ACCESS GOD

One of the things you discover in the pigsty is the grace of prayer. Prayer is not done in a hurry; you have to slow yourself down. The pigsty took me out of the routine rat race of the environment, and sat me down. Prayer changed from the usual recitations into a dynamic communication tool between the eternal Divine and me. Only God could reach out deep, wide and far enough. Everything and everyone else had given up on me; at least that was how I saw it. When I reached out to God in prayer, I heard him say, *"I will never leave you, or forsake you."*

For the most part, I read the bible from a theology perspective—understanding God within the limitations of my environment. That paradigm shifted; I began to understand God within the unlimited scope of God's eternalness.

In God's eternalness, I was lifted up into his divine context. I no longer saw God from an earthly perspective, but saw the earth from a God perspective. In the former I stood within my situation; in the latter I stood above it. Looking at my situation from above gave me a clearer and more realistic view—the higher I went in prayer, the smaller the problem became. My environment did not change, just my perception of it.

Our anxieties are caused more by perception than by reality. Two people can be exposed to the same situation, and yet react differently—the one totally berserk, the other may remain calm. Personal vision depends on how big or small you perceive God to be.

Paul wrote, Ephesians 3:20 (The Message) *"God can do anything, you know—far more than you could ever imagine, or guess, or request in your wildest dreams!"* There are no limits to what God can do through one person totally yielded to God and his purpose. That's a frightening thing to know, it makes you look around and wonder why most of us settle for mediocrity when there is so much power buried in our innermost. The possibilities of being powerful in God are immense and beyond measure; and the challenge of all living is daring those possibilities.

We all know that tired cliché, "The sky is the limit". Modern engineering has taken us way beyond that thinking. Today we penetrate the skies and discover millions upon millions of stars, planets and galaxies we never knew existed. The wide distances in the universe are only an ocean drop compared to what eternalness is like; you search and push for the edge towards an ever-widening horizon. The sky is no longer the limit.

Once we begin the journey into God's eternalness, there is no turning back in this pilgrimage where you arrive, yet never arrive. That journey begins now! If you understand the demands of the journey, then you know there is no time to look over your shoulder wondering how far back others are or how further along you may be. You just hit the road in the best way you know how—and keep going!

THE PRICE ALWAYS GOES BEFORE THE PRIZE

When Nelson Mandela determined in his heart to pursue the struggle for the liberation of black people in South Africa, it was more than just a cause—it was a passion. A worthy cause demands conviction, otherwise the temptation to give up sets in as the process unfolds. Mandela as a young lawyer saw the prize, and had no illusions about the price—that was the matter with him. In his well-known closing argument during the Rivonia trial, he made that abundantly clear to the presiding judge:

"During my lifetime, I have dedicated myself to this struggle of the African people. I have fought against white domination, and I have fought against black domination. I have cherished the ideal of a democratic and free society in which all persons live together in harmony and with equal opportunities. It is an ideal, which I hope to live for and to achieve. But if needs be, it is an ideal for which I am prepared to die."

After I had understood that my "who am I" can only be defined meaningfully in the context of "whose am I", a further question was answered, "What am I here for?" The answer to Warren's question just slid into place. When the whole story of life is eventually told, it will be about return on investment, not how many people hurt me, what degrees I hold, whether I have ever met the president of my country, what the balance of my account is—or a host of similar questions that left me spinning with anxiety.

That was a powerful insight, and immediately a sigh of relief poured out of me. I didn't have to be so stressed trying to please the world at my expense—almost to the brink of insanity. I accepted without question the Master's invitation, *Matthew 11:28* "*Come to me, all you who are weary and burdened, and I will give you rest.*"

Much of what we do in a cut-throat world, we do to gain the approval of others. We seem to forget that the earth is already turning and we don't have to spin it. These esteem games we play often come at a cost steeper than we are willing to admit or pay, for that matter. Eventually, we lose the very life we are trying to save.

The universe is a big place to find anything; it was easier finding a needle in a haystack. The small voice continued, "Something in the universe is the matter with you, and only you." I wanted to run and find some way of pushing time back—just to give myself enough space to find it. Jesus called it, *"The Kingdom of God in you."*

A GIFT OF THE GIVEN

Gifts are original—giving back what you were given to the best of your ability. The beauty of your gift is its uniqueness because it is born from within; it is a vigorous engagement with the dynamism of your own spirit. Good art is capturing the synthesis of that tension, putting it on canvas, and then giving it to God and the universe—it is your unique contribution.

If your gift is your highest calling, it must eventually turn heads, because it fits like a perfect shoe. If you limp your way to greatness, check the size of your feet, or the size of your shoes. You don't have to have festering blisters to achieve greatness: do what you do, in the best way you know how.

Gifts, in their rareness, have a way of blessing the earth and all who live in it, and when the seed sprouts, you are immediately ushered into greatness. A wise man said, *Proverbs 18:16* *"A gift opens the way for the giver and ushers him into the presence of the great."* Greatness that is sought is often buried with your bones, but greatness that seeks after you lives on long after you are gone. It just doesn't come cheap.

I looked at what I had; nothing was new, but it took on a completely different meaning. I didn't have to go hunting all over the universe looking for what I didn't know; I just had to explore what I had in a more meaningful way.

When that truth landed, a whole eternity opened up before my eyes. For the first time, I understood what Christ meant when he spoke about eternal life—life that lives on when everything else physical around you collapses. I didn't have to fly away on some glad morning to live life in the fullest; it began right there and then.

When I gained that eternal and cosmic perspective of things, I felt like some magi from the east was imparting words of wisdom into my spirit, *"In all your seeking, seek to fulfil the purpose for which you were created."*

Purpose is your reason to live, and if need be, your reason to die. It is that one meaningful, spiritual and universal aspiration and inspiration which you are driven in your deepest being to pursue until the end of time and beyond. It adds value not only to self, but to others as well. It stretches from birth to death in that lifelong learning challenge of climbing towards a destiny that beckons beyond the horizon.

Right there, I called off every other search and focused on finding what was the matter with me—it was an invitation with a promise, *Matthew 6:33(NIV)* *"But seek first his kingdom and his righteousness, and all these things will be given to you as well."* I began the journey I thought I had been in all along.

Christ's death on the cross was not an isolated action focused on a tiny speck in the universe—he was effectively returning us to the beginning. We are part of a larger whole; and life on earth is meaningful to the extent that we live it to the fullest in relation to the whole. As the Teacher said, *John 10:10* *"I have come that they may have life, and have it to the full."*

When our relationship with God was disrupted in the Garden of Eden, we were plunged deep into the waters of human anxiety—and now we must swim. It's hard work swimming in those unpredictable waters—we drown, we are drowned and we drown others. Those who make it to some imaginary "finish line" reach it, muscles aching, worn out. It is all in the rat race of wondering what the forbidden fruit tastes like—and our little wonders turn into dizzying and confusing action. Just enjoy what you were given, and find ways of sharing it with others.

THE HORSE MUST COME BEFORE THE CART

Riders in chariots of war knew they had to get one thing straight: the horse must come before the cart. If a fighter got that order mixed up, he was as good as dead. Doing things right the first time increases your chances of success. If you rig the process, you may get away with it the first time, or even a second time, but eventually someone will sense that you are a fraud.

Anxiety will often push us to seek the easy way out, we are occupied by necessary run-off-the-mill issues, and we spend the rest of our lives putting food on the table and hunting for shelter. Most of it is good— but is it meaningful? Can we look back at the end of time, and pat ourselves on the back for a life well lived?

Frankl affirms that real meaning goes beyond food, shelter, beverage and the finer things in life. Jesus taught a similar principle in various ways: ^{Luke 4:4} *"It is written: 'Man does not live on bread alone'."* Frankl's experiences in the Nazi death camps convinced him that the human being's desire to live for something beyond himself is often enough to submerge the person in an unquenchable passion for and pursuit of a more meaningful life.

If you chase wealth, it often demands your health; but, if you stay with what you know best, wealth follows as a matter of fact. ^{Proverbs 10:22} *"The blessing of the LORD brings wealth, and he adds no trouble to it."* Wealth must come as a reward, not in pursuit of happiness.

The ultimate in life is to search deep within us for purpose beyond the average. The Kingdom of God in its vastness, tendency, power and prowess is the constant pursuit for higher aspirations in the context of God's overall purpose for the universe.

Adam and Eve were charged with keeping the Garden of Eden; providence and provision belonged to God—until they believed truth at its twisted point. Peter was fine walking on water until he became realistic with his surroundings—and then his anxieties began. If we remove our eyes from *The Truth,* we are always ensnared by the twist in what seems truthful.

In prayer, we pool our inner resources to focus on who God has destined for us to be. God is not preoccupied with who we are, who we think we are, or who others think we are. The question that begs our most urgent attention is, "Who in God are we becoming?" The answer will unfold differently from one person to another, and from one level to another within each person—that is a lifetime occupation.

God is the rainmaker, not the clouds

People who read radar screens have an amazing ability to distinguish *noise* from *signal.* Their eyes and ears are trained to identify the slightest foreign element right through the blurring noises off their screens. The worst and costly mistake is to identify *signal* as *noise,* because the enemy might land on your doorstep very unexpectedly.

Our assurances in God's will are not always introduced by the rumbling of a thunderstorm. They are found in the gentle whisper that comes through loud and clear in the midst of all the blurring noise that surrounds us.

Sometimes we look for God in all the wrong places: the windstorm, earthquake, fire, only to discover that he comes through in a gentle whisper. We are fooled by the euphoria of the moment; we think God is housed in buildings of marble and the high sounds of sophisticated musical instruments, only to discover later and much further along that we were embracing a whirlwind.

When Elijah started announcing that rain was coming, the clouds were not dark and heavy with rain—his servant reported seeing a cloud the size of a man's hand. After three and a half years of drought, that was not much to scream about. The weather bureau would have dismissed his announcement with contempt. Elijah warned Ahab to start preparing, otherwise he would be caught up in the rain. He believed in the rainmaker, not the cloud—showers of blessings come from beyond the clouds.

IT CAN BE A WET EXPERIENCE WITHOUT AN UMBRELLA!

Anybody caught unprepared on a rainy day knows what a miserable and wet experience it can be. In a city with poor control systems, the waters run wasted down the streets and soon evaporate into the air. Farmers know how to prepare for rain; they have various forms of equipment to ensure that the water is stored up and put to good use.

Some breakthroughs come in abundance, only to find us unprepared, and we miss great experiences because we were not ready. Breakthroughs are more meaningful when we are prepared for them, body, soul and spirit. Elijah physically outran Ahab's chariots (physical preparation). He was convinced in his mind (psychological preparation) that God had answered his prayer. When his spiritual sustenance dried up, and he lay under the solitary broom tree asking to die, God lifted him up and set him on the road again. He depended exclusively on God for his spiritual refill (spiritual preparation).

Our experiences through the wilderness and on the mountaintop require an alignment of our total selves. Once we are scattered all over the place we lose the coherence and effectiveness of a unit that must function as one. If it's the last thing we do, we need to find our place in the universe.

IF GOD IS IN IT, IT DOESN'T MATTER HOW STUPID IT SOUNDS OR LOOKS!

Jesus once told a story (Luke 11:5-13) of a man who had an unexpected hungry visitor in the middle of the night and he had nothing to offer him. If you have seen the look on a hungry man's face, then you understand why the man Jesus spoke about had to go knocking at the shopkeeper's door at midnight.

Business people work according to business hours, and naturally the shopkeeper was not amused by a knock so late in the night for one loaf of bread—it was just not worth the trouble. He could sell more loaves in his waking hours. He told the man to go away, but the man would not move. Shamelessly he stood at the door, and just kept knocking; it did not matter what the shopkeeper thought about him, or what curses he was pronouncing, he was going to wait until that door opened even if the heavens had to come crashing down.

Finally the shopkeeper, furious and annoyed, got up and gave him what he needed; he did not care one bit about him, all he wanted was for him to go away. The hungry man did go away—but not until his hands were full.

In the end, it has to come. If God is in it, it doesn't matter how stupid it looks, otherwise it is ridiculously stupid. Who can feed five thousand people on a few loaves and two fish, who can turn water into wine? Who can walk on water and not drown? Who can call a little girl back from the dead?

The man knocking on the shopkeeper's door was persistent, resolved and focused. No amount of ridicule was going to drive him away from the only place his need would be met. There was no way in the whole world he could go back home empty-handed. He just kept knocking, and he knew that the only thing standing between supply and demand was a piece of crafted wood. In his determination, he was not going to move until that door swung wide open.

When I rose from the pigsty, I was hungry, but I also knew there were millions of others hidden in the dark night. They were just as hungry, if not worse; and I knew where to find *the bread of life*. I was tired of half-baked half-loaves, and in my deepest being, I yearned for God's real thing—again. I knew many who were promised a full belly, only for their tummies to be filled with sand.

My turn to knock at the Master's door had come, and it came with a promise, ^{Revelation 3:8b} *"See, I have placed before you an open door that no one can shut. I know that you have little strength, yet you have kept my word and have not denied my name."*

Our breakthrough in prayer is sure if we keep on knocking, if we keep on seeking, if we keep on asking—that was the shamelessness demonstrated by the man, and he walked away with his hands full. If you resolve to stay with God, you must come back with a testimony.

YOU MAY BE GOD'S SHOWSTOPPER!

If you want to get the big picture straight, focus on the small pictures that make up the big one: each picture is a full picture in its own right.

God is working out the details. We are often pressed for the big picture, we want the full pattern now when God is still piecing it all together. Fashion designers don't get to parade their pieces before they are sown together; they parade a finished product, and the showstopper always comes last. You may be God's showstopper! Give it your best shot each day as if it were your last.

EPILOGUE

Don't be afraid!

*¹Jn 4:18 "There is no fear in love. But perfect love drives out fear,
because fear has to do with punishment.
The one who fears is not made perfect in love."*

The world is driven by fear more than we care to admit. We are not only afraid of each other, we are afraid of ourselves. We build nuclear armaments with a capacity to wipe ourselves out, and call it protection or defence, but the truth is, we are afraid. We defend the greed in others that we see so clearly in ourselves.

Fear is as old as human existence. When God called out to Adam in the Garden of Eden, his response was, *Genesis 3:10 (NIV) "I heard you in the garden, and I was afraid because I was naked; so I hid."* The question was clear, *"Why are you not where I created you to be?"*

The chief objective in writing this book was to facilitate a process in which the reader can return to the beginning—the real beginning. The biggest temptation is to climb a ladder leaning against the wrong wall, because you must protect your territory. If you are where you shouldn't be, fear is the order of the day.

STAY THE CAUSE!

When I grew up, our street did not have lights. One day I went running into the dark, and suddenly something white and screaming appeared, and it was rushing towards me—I panicked, and my knees literally starting wobbling as I hit the ground. One of the boys had decided to cover himself with a white sheet, and he scared me so badly, I turned purple with fear—I couldn't move.

Frankly, there is no such thing as a fearless state. The bravest among us is afraid, and the most fearful can be daring. When I sat in the pigsty fear was my constant torment; everything around me said, "You are finished." For as long as I believed that, I couldn't move.

Fear removes your focus from what can be to what is. It says to you, "There is no bread for you—the shopkeeper is sleeping; stop seeking, knocking, or asking. Just go away!" I couldn't afford that; even if it was the last prayer I prayed on earth.

If you are afraid, you are effectively blinding yourself to opportunities around you, because your eyes are looking at your surroundings; you seal your fate in a self-created mummy box—a memory of what could have been. People will only see what you looked like, until you died alive.

FEAR IS A STATE OF MIND

Like everything else, fear is a state of mind. I was in the pigsty long before I landed in there—in my mind at least. Earning a salary was the only way I thought I could sustain our family life, and losing my job was a terrifying contemplation. One day as I stood outside the house admiring my new car, something said, "A dark wave is coming, and it is going to sweep away all this excitement you have." I was extremely afraid; I could not imagine life without my idols.

That voice of doom was so clear in my spirit, it wiped off my smile. I started chanting positive "confessions" to redirect those approaching shadowy forces away from me. A few months later, the first episode of doom started rolling out. Virtually all my fears started happening—one after another. I landed squarely in the places I feared most. Job expressed a similar feeling when he said, *Job 3:25(NIV)* *"What I feared has come upon me; what I dreaded has happened to me."*

I still did a lot of God-talk, but God had become a lucky charm for desperate moments. Everything was about me, and how the earth and all who live in it could benefit me. Such a world wasn't completely meaningful for me—I still missed something bigger, but I was afraid of losing that smaller picture.

When I lost everything, I had nothing to lose anymore; even my fear had to go. I had to start thinking differently about everything, even the fear that paralysed me. Two things were clear in the pigsty—either I settled in with the pigs, or I found my way out. I chose to come out, some of the sty stench still hung on me, but I was coming out—it was another state of mind.

Nothing happens until it all gets sorted out in your mind—the *metanoia* experience. That "mind" thing is repeated in biblical scripture from many directions—that's where it all begins. I switched the fear in my mind for the love of God. If you sweep your house clean, something new must replace the old, otherwise the old invites other homeless demons to occupy your clean house, and your current state becomes worse than the previous.

When I looked at myself in the pigsty, something kept reminding me of the stench; and who wants a pig? People love pork and all that, but no one wants to keep a pig for company—except other pigs. And the nasty voice kept coming, "Once a pig, always a pig." I had to choose whether to believe it or not.

My mind kept playing around with the thought of being loved again—uncompromising love that could find its way through the stench and the muddy clay in the sty. That love would have to be more than natural; I loved my bit, and was loved back—and naturally, all I came out with was pain. I gave some, I received some. There had to be something different.

As I reached out to God in Christ, that picture began to shift; I began to feel the warmth of his love by faith—pure lavished unlimited love with no hint of reproof or spite. When I understood—even in the smallest way—that God loved me, my fears began to melt. Love, like fear, is a state of mind.

When you know and feel genuinely loved, you can't be afraid anymore. As John the apostle said, [1Jn 4:18] " . . . *perfect love drives out fear . . . .*" Psychiatrists are now playing around with the concept of *LOVE*. As can be expected, it remains a profound and elusive mystery. Love *(agape)* cannot be separated from God, because God is Love.

Breaking with the past is not easy, especially if you keep looking over your shoulder. There are many forces that call you back into the rut; you remember the good times in bad places. When you reach that point, the temptation to return to what you know is great; especially if you look for miles ahead, and all you can see is lifeless and dreary wasteland—no bees for honey, or cows for milk.

When you set out on a journey into the unknown, it feels very alone—not lonely, just alone. You walk out of a kind of bondage into a liberating solo experience—straight into a strait with God. You walk, not because you see, but because you know. You begin the journey armed with nothing but a vision and a miracle-working God.

LET GOD BE GOD!

Setting out on a wilderness journey is naturally a frightening experience, especially if you want some guarantees—there are none; and that's the place to start. The wilderness is about releasing your creative spirit, and daring to retrieve from your innermost being your songs of deliverance. Each one of us is a gift to the earth, and when we let it out, we return to God what God gave to us.

A MIRACLE-WORKING GOD

The whole bible is an undisputed story of a miracle-working God. Jesus told the doubting crowds of his time, [John 10:38] *"But if I do his work, believe in the evidence of the miraculous works I have done . . ."* The apostles also prayed, *Acts 4:30 "Stretch out your hand with healing power, may miraculous signs and wonders be done through the name of your holy servant Jesus."* Every miracle in scripture is a demonstration of the power of God, and a challenge to unbelief. John the apostle said a mouthful when he wrote, *John 20:30 "The disciples saw Jesus do many miraculous signs in addition to the ones recorded in this book. But these are written so that you may continue to believe that Jesus is the Messiah the Son of God."*

He recorded eight miraculous signs among many, and all of them intended so that people may believe in Jesus. That is the precise intention of miracles, to help us understand that nothing is impossible with God. The challenge is to move our focus from the mountain to the maker of the mountain.

We need to commit not to the miracle, but to the maker of the miracle. The eight miracles recorded in the book of John demonstrate different aspects of God's supernatural power. In every case the situation was beyond human intervention. The people involved wouldn't have done anything about their crises; only a miracle would save their day! A miracle is a miracle with us, but with God, it is business as usual.

BETTER THE BITTER OF FIRST EXPERIENCES

The first miracle in the New Testament was performed in Galilee. The wedding must have attracted everybody from around the tiny village of Cana. The couple must have done their best to prepare, not so much for themselves, but for the invited guests, and naturally, the highest items on their to-do list must have included getting good food and quality wine. Those two items are not negotiable in a wedding celebration. In the context of that world, no celebration of any kind was worth any serious consideration without wine, good wine first and then the other wine.

Such occasions attracted everybody to come out; for some it provided a grand opportunity to gather around and gossip. The man in charge of the feast had to be an expert in wine tasting, and it proved to be true at this wedding. What wedding is a wedding without wine? The whisperers from around town were there; no doubt, the story would circulate everywhere. The couple would have been accused of anything from poor planning, to biting off more than they could chew.

Some people are gifted in making matters worse, they specialise in stirring fires where they already exist, or in starting them where there are none, just to make trouble for you. It's not enough that you have your hands full; otherwise, it would make theirs look empty. This lot is never absent from any crisis; in the townships of South Africa, every celebration has a mad person who moves attention from the beauty of the bride and the groom to his or her own lunacy.

Crisis situations need a perceptive mind, one that cautiously separates sense from nonsense. Mary the mother of Jesus had one such mind, and she knew just what to do about the crisis. Perception is a deep and calculated response to problem solving, an involvement that seeks to add value when all others lose their heads.

Jesus saved the situation; he turned water into wine, good wine, better than what the host had offered. The expert tasted it, and nobody stood up to oppose his affirmation; the second wine was better than the first in a very unusual sequence of events.

The miracle here was the quality of the wine. Jesus did not follow the known processes of winemaking. You don't need not be an expert to know that at least you need grapes, and some period to allow the process of fermentation in winemaking. But here, water instantly changed to quality wine. Not even a minute allowed for fermentation.

That is what miracles are all about—impossible from a human point of view, and possible only with God. Physical science in all its glory will never claim such an achievement; at the very least, they can only dismiss it as nonsensical. But what god would be God if he were trapped in the confines of laboratory analysis?

This situation at the wedding was desperate because there was no way out, all known and existing resources had been exhausted, and the couple had their backs against the wall. In one way or another, we have all been there. You give the situation your best shot, but it's just not good enough—until God comes along and introduces your breakthrough; a one hundred and one per cent miracle in all its fullness, with no room for the slightest jot of doubt.

GOD WILL COVER GREAT DISTANCES TO DELIVER YOUR MIRACLE

Jesus performed his second miracle in the same area where the first one took place, and this time for a Roman official. Jews and Romans weren't the best of friends in those days. In fact, more than anything else the Jews wanted a Messiah who would help them overthrow the Roman regime. But when you are in a tight corner, it really doesn't matter where your help comes from, but it had better be good, especially where sceptic opposition is involved.

The Roman official's son was dying and he was certainly in no mood for jokes. He came to Jesus because he desperately needed an answer, and time was running out. Jesus sent him home where his miracle was waiting. The boy was healed at the precise moment that Jesus said he would be; again, there were witnesses to this effect. The challenge here was space, where Jesus was and where the miracle took place. In performing this miracle, Jesus established himself as Lord over space. No distance can stand between God and your miracle; prayer is the critical link between the two. With God, distance is not a hurdle.

The Roman official, in his own way, probably expected a more dignified response, but he did not ask questions when Jesus said, *"Go back home, your son will live!"* John 4:50 *" . . . [T]he man believed what Jesus said and started home."* Great miracles are always preceded by faith; nothing happens if we don't believe. The Gospel of John has three words at the centre of its theme: miracle, believe and life, and in almost every confrontation, the challenge is to believe.

No miracle stands alone; all of them are intended to direct people to God, and thus impart life. Faith is the livewire that connects us to a living God, because the person who comes to God by faith must also believe in God's eternal existence. Our trust and commitment are established in the sure fact that when we pray, God hears and answers our prayer. The space between where we are and where God is, is not a problem—God will cover great distances to deliver your miracle.

NO CRUMBS OF PITY ANYMORE!

A man crippled for thirty-eight years once lay beside a pool in Bethesda (John 5:1-9), and for thirty-eight years he tried to drag himself into the healing waters, and every time others overtook him.

Thirty-eight years is a very long time for anyone to be sick, especially if you see hope just a few metres away. This happened in Jerusalem, the religious centre of those times, but none of the people considered helping him even for a split second. He lay there year after excruciating year, and others kept snatching what could have been his miracle. But then, Jesus came along, and thirty-eight years' worth of plain pain and misery were resolved in an instant.

The beauty of this miracle is that it was beyond dispute—there was no challenging its integrity and genuineness—it was perfect from all dimensions. It had to be perfect, otherwise the religious leaders of the day would be only too happy to expose its loophole.

God's interventions are beyond question, that's why when you have your miracle people search dead waters for live fish, just to remove attention from what God is doing. This miracle in particular was for the religious crowds. The crippled man did not even know who Jesus was. The religious leaders held on to a form of religion but denied its power.

The tragedy of all religion is its two-facedness and fraudulence, always marching in pious self-assurance and parading in fakeness that feeds on human applause. It's amazing how we enjoy seeing others in defenceless positions. When the once-crippled man started walking around enjoying his miracle, the only thing the Pharisees could see was a mat he carried on a Sabbath. It was okay with them when he just lay there for thirty-eight long years, and all they did was throw crumbs of pity at him; at least they had some form of advantage over his life.

When their power base was punctured, they had to find another way to keep him down. Sure, he was carrying a mat on a Sabbath, but there was something bigger at work here, and as usual, they missed it.

God is always doing something new, and we miss it simply because we hang on to some moth-eaten self-righteous perception. We twist God's arm and expect him to operate within our rigid and morose religious prescriptions. In the process we miss out on the real and big thing. If people point at your old mat, give it to them and enjoy your miracle.

THE DEEPER INTO THE WATERS, THE DEEPER THE PRAYER

The disciples had several experiences with rough seas, and they were delivered in every instance. One evening Jesus insisted that they go ahead of him to Capernaum, and he remained on a nearby hill to pray. About five kilometres into the rough seas, the situation became worse, and the disciples knew they were in deep trouble in the deep waters. Jesus came to the rescue walking on the water, and the troubled sea subsided. They reached land safely, and they did not understand how, just as they did not understand the feeding of the five thousand. The miracle is not *what* happened, it's *how* it happened. The deeper we go into the turbulent ocean of faith, the more intense our prayers must become.

"COME AND WALK THE WATERS WITH ME!"

When God calls us into abundant life in Jesus Christ, it comes with a vision. In God's vision, he extends the invitation, *"Come, and walk the waters with me"*, and for as long as our eyes are kept on God, we will walk the waters confidently and triumphantly. Peter flunked the test, and he sank. Any vision worthy of a dignified feat stands waiting on the other side of the rough waters. Our biggest challenge is to traverse the gap between where we are and where we want to be with penetrating focus on the one who bids us to come.

The mountain may be full of hazards, and many lives may have been lost before—it happens all the time on Mt. Everest—but we must walk the deepest waters and climb the highest peaks. We are admonished, ^{Zechariah 4:6}*"Not by might, nor by power, but by my spirit said the Lord."* At one point Peter sank because he took his eyes off the one who calls. ^{Hebrews 12:2(NIV)} *"Let us fix our eyes on Jesus, the author and perfecter of our faith, who for the joy set before him endured the cross, scorning its shame, and sat down at the right hand of the throne of God."*

IT DOESN'T RUN IN THE FAMILY

Jesus and his disciples once came across a blind man, and immediately the disciples asked, ^{John 9: 1-3} *"Why was this man born blind? Was it because of his own sins, or his parents' sins?"* And Jesus answered, *"It was not because of his sins or his parents' sins, this happened so the power of God could be seen in him."* That question is very typical of how we think, which is that nothing just happens.

I'm sure this was not a question on the minds only of the disciples; this blind man and his guilt-ridden parents must have gone through some of the most frustrating times trying to understand what had happened, or wondering whether somebody somewhere in the distant past just did not do the right thing. "Maybe it runs in the family" is something they may have thought. "Maybe this is a curse from other generations . . ."

In Africa, anything is possible; people blame their miseries on anything and anybody. A man blamed his brother of witchcraft because he had disabled children. Another accused his mother of killing his family and cursing his business. That attitude was not developed yesterday—it runs all the way back to when Adam blamed Eve, and Cain killed Abel. When blame and jealousy mature, murder is born. If you blame something or someone for your misery, you are permanently disabled. You miss the opportunity to identify how you relate to your problem, and the only truth that could turn you around is buried forever.

The answers to our future don't necessarily lie in a foggy past. With God in the picture, all curses have run their last mile, and what lies ahead is open ground. Like Jeremiah (12:25), we get set to "*run with the horses*" and to invade the "*thickets of the Jordan*".

THE PAST MUST NOT CURSE THE FUTURE

One of the greatest setbacks in the achievement of vision is to be trapped in past failures you may not even have been part of. There is nothing as frustrating as a futile search because in the end you come up with nothing constructive, it's like fishing in lifeless waters.

The blind man had not sinned, neither had his parents. There was another reason for his blindness, entirely different from what everybody else thought, and perhaps one which no one wanted to consider. Sometimes the answer is found in the issues we sweep beneath the carpet. If we bring out into the open what we are hiding in our innermost beings, it may just be the key to greater things.

A very difficult thing to do is maintain focus in a blaming culture. It's easier to point fingers than to acknowledge our own wrongdoing, if any. One way to move forward is to acknowledge our own contribution to a miserable past, and use that as a jumpstart to greater achievements. Our destiny is in the hands of God, and God alone, and once we establish that in our minds, there is no force strong enough to pull us back. There is no demon potent enough to destroy the purpose of God about anything.

The beauty of a beckoning future is that it offers a blank sheet, and the opportunity to rewrite our story, a brand new story.

FROM THE STENCH OF DEATH COMES LIFE

The resurrection of Lazarus is an amazing story of victory over death. He lay in the grave for four days, and Jesus came along and called him back into life (John 11:1-44). When Lazarus died, Jesus was not in the vicinity, and both Martha and Mary expressed regret, *"Lord, if only you would have been here, my brother wouldn't have died."* Martha believed in the resurrection, but only as a future experience, but Jesus promised as in now, *"Your brother will rise again."*

It happens all too often that when people die they take us along with them. We may be alive, but a big part of us is buried with our loved one because they were a significant part of our lives. When they die all life loses meaning because in a sense they had become our idols, perhaps even taking the place of God. Only Jesus is Lord over all, and in the death of others, we need to find our own resurrection.

Death is a painful experience for those who lose their loved ones, and like everybody who is desperate, Mary and Martha weren't about to entertain heartless jokes. The loss had them crying the whole time—as a matter of fact, the whole village joined in their grief. For everybody else, Lazarus was dead, but for Jesus, *"It happened for the glory of God so that the Son of God will receive his glory from this."* The death of Lazarus was not just another death: God had a Purpose. When Jesus finally called, *"'Lazarus come out!' The dead man came out, his hands and feet bound in graveclothes, his face wrapped in a headcloth."* And Jesus said, *"unwrap him, and let him go."* Lazarus lived even though he was dead. He walked out leaving the stench of death in his grave. Some situations must die a natural death before a new life can emerge.

This miracle was a forerunner to a mysterious and profound truth, ^{John 11:25} *"Jesus said to her, "I am the resurrection and the life. He who believes in me will live, even though he dies."* Jesus obviously communicated at a different level than was familiar; even more than physical resurrection, he referred to eternal life. In the Christ sense, you are not alive just because you breathe and go about your everyday routine with no commitment to God, because then you are dead even though you are alive. A rich life is in living and believing that Christ is the Son of God, because then you live even though you were dead.

COME OUT!

In the jungles of Africa, there is only one rule: survival of the fittest. And every animal is built to survive the stiff competition for existence. It comes with the territory, you grab first, or someone else will take what could have been yours. There is enough for everyone, but some of us just seem to enjoy hoarding more than others, even if it goes to waste. An animal that is not out there in the open is not likely to identify opportunities for a kill, and if that goes on long enough, it's as good as dead, stone dead! It can't stay hidden in the bushes forever in that world of "kill or be killed"; it must come out!

Not so long ago I dealt with a teenager who is HIV positive; she sat in a dark corner and with a hopeless look on her face, she was obviously waiting to die. "There is no hope," she said, "How am I ever going to face the world again?" She had a lot on her mind, and the more she thought about her situation, the nearer and deeper she got into her grave. She was buried already because she died many times before her actual death.

In situations like that, we often remind people of the story of Lazarus. With Jesus around, nobody deserves to remain in the grave, however long they have been there. In the valley of death, Jesus called Martha's brother by name, *"Lazarus, Come out!"* This whole thing was not about the world; it was about Lazarus, the world just came to witness the new "madness" in town.

The crowd that stood at the burial site had never seen anything like that before, it was brand new and powerful, and only God deserved the glory. The HIV-positive teenager was worried about the world, but this was about her and her resurrection from the dead. She was dead, yet alive. We tried to make her realise that if she remained in her "grave", neither she nor the world would ever know what could have become of her in God's Purpose.

People are buried in many and different ways by many and different situations, and the world hurries to issue death certificates because they want to help themselves to what used to be yours. Jesus dealt the greedy a terrible blow; Lazarus rose from the dead and occupied his rightful place in the land of the living.

If we remain buried in hopelessness it serves no good to anyone. Not many people care if you are dead or alive, they have their own graves to worry about. So if you dare to live again, make the most of it to the glory of God.

Lazarus rose from the dead just when everybody else had closed every chapter on his life. He was stone dead, a total write-off, never to be seen again on the face of the earth; for some he would exist only as a memory. Until Jesus came along and called his name from among the dead, and the dead man walked out of his grave to embrace a second chance in life.

He knows your name

God knows your name; that was a very comforting thought when everybody else forgot my name. I wasn't too sure what my name was either because I have different names on my paternal and maternal sides. I just settled with the one that everybody knew—but God knows every name I have. He knew and called many people by their first names, Adam, Abram, Samuel, Saul of Tarsus. He knows your name—no matter how unintelligible you may think it is.

Jesus ordered the stone to be removed and called Lazarus by name, but Lazarus had to take the steps to come out. No one rushed in there to help him out; they did not believe it possible in the first place; he responded, not with a shout back, but with action. It was incumbent upon him to walk back into the resurrection life that stood calling outside his grave.

Faith is always accompanied by action in the direction of God's calling. Otherwise, you stay wrapped up in the grave. Come out! Death does not recognise itself until life comes along.

When we give up all hope about anything we effectively give up on life. Hope is possible for just as long as we breathe, and it's always the bright light at the end of a dark tunnel. Sometimes there is no light and we can't even tell whether the tunnel ends. Right there it feels like the end has come, and yet even there we can still hope against all hope, *Romans 4:18* "*Against all hope, Abraham in hope believed and so became the father of many nations, just as it had been said to him, 'So shall your offspring be'.*"

When Abraham and Sarah gave birth to Isaac there was no hope; they were both well beyond child-bearing age. God is always inviting us to hope, *Zechariah 9:12* "*Return to your fortress, O prisoners of hope; even now I announce that I will restore twice as much to you.*"

Hope is fearless because it marches against hope to mount the insurmountable. Essentially, it is at peace with itself because it cannot be threatened by the fraudulence of the environment. As Nelson Mandela said, "*If you are in harmony with yourself, you may meet a lion without fear, because he respects anyone with self-confidence*" (Crwys-Williams, 1997:74).

REFERENCES

Buber, M. (trans. Smith, R.). (1984. Reprint). *I and thou*. Edinburgh: T & T Clark.

Cannan, E. (Ed.) (1994). *Adam Smith: The wealth of nations*. New York: The Modern Library.

Clinebell, H.J. (1975). *Growth Counseling for marriage enrichment*. Fortress Press. Philadelphia

Clinebell, H.J., and Clinebell, C.H. (1970). *The intimate marriage*. San Francisco: Harper and Row.

Covey, S.R. (1989). *The 7 habits of highly effective people*. London: Simon & Schuster.

Crwys-Williams, J. (1997). *In the words of Nelson Mandela*. Johannesburg: Penguin Books.

Frankl, V.E. (1984). *Man's search for meaning*. New York: Pocket Books.

Healy, K.M. (2004). *From beholding to becoming*. Grand Rapids, Michigan: Brazos Press.

Karasu, T.B. (2003). The art of serenity: The path to a joyful life in the best and worst of times. New York: Simon & Schuster.

Meredith, M. (1997). *Nelson Mandela: A biography*. Middlesex, England: Penguin Books.

Moltmann, J. (1978). The open church: Invitation to a messianic lifestyle. London: SCM Press.

Peck, M.S. (1978). *The road less travelled*. London: Rider.

Pussey, E. (Revision of English translation). (1996). *The confessions of Saint Augustine*. New Kensington, PA: Whitaker House.

Sacks, O. (1970). *The man who mistook his wife for a hat*. New York: Harper & Row.

Senge, P.M. (1990). The fifth discipline: The art and practice of a learning organisation. London: Random House.

Warren, R. (2002). *The purpose driven life*. Grand Rapids, Michigan: Zondervan.

White, J. (1982). The mask of melancholy: A Christian psychiatrist looks at depression and suicide. Glasgow: Inter-varsity Press.

ABOUT THE AUTHOR

Steve Mochechane is a pastor and teacher for many years. His ministerial career includes pastoring in different parts of South Africa. He was a high school teacher, and spent some time lecturing in a school of theology.

He spent more than ten years in the corporate world as an HRD specialist. His area of interest is personal and corporate transformation, and leadership development.

He received his B.A. degree from ICI University once based in Brussels, Belgium, and currently operating from Irving, Texas (USA). He was awarded a scholarship by the Educational Opportunities Council in Johannesburg to pursue graduate studies at Garret Evangelical Theological Seminary (Northwestern University) in Evanston, Illinois.